LAURIE SHARMA

ISBN: 978-1-7363670-0-1

Copyright 2022 © by Laurie Sharma

PROLOGUE

There is a reason why you are reading this book.
There are no mistakes and it's not a coincidence.
You are special. You have been set apart. You have been chosen, selected and hand-picked for this very moment.
Whether you choose to accept it or not, there is a new and exciting plan for your life that is about to unfold.
So sit back, and get ready to enjoy your life's new journey!

TABLE OF CONTENTS

Introduction	SPIRITUAL CANCER	7
Chapter 1	SPIRITUAL CANCER: THE DISEASE	11
Chapter 2	BORN THIS WAY	15
Chapter 3	NEW AGE, PSYCHICS AND RELIGION	27
Chapter 4	ABSOLUTE TRUTH vs. RELATIVE TRUTH	33
Chapter 5	IS SCIENCE PROOF OF GOD?	39
Chapter 6	TIME IS MONEY	55
Chapter 7	CONTROL OR NO CONTROL? THAT IS THE QUESTION	63
Chapter 8	UNAWARE OF HIS PRESENCE	73
Chapter 9	TEXT MESSAGE FROM GOD	87
Chapter 10	THE CURE	99
Chapter 11	RELIGION vs. RELATIONSHIP	115
Chapter 12	SPIRITUAL WARFARE THE HIDDEN BATTLE	133

Chapter 13	**STRENGTHENING** YOUR **SPIRITUAL MUSCLES** **145**
Chapter 14	**WHY** DO **BAD THINGS HAPPEN** TO **GOOD PEOPLE** **165**
Chapter 15	**FACT IS STRANGER** THAN **FICTION** **177**
Chapter 16	**CHOOSING LIFE** OR **DEATH** **187**
Chapter 17	**SUPERHERO** VS. **SAVIOR** **201**
Endnotes	.... **218**
Acknowledgements	.... **219**
About the Author	.... **223**
Contemporary Christian Music Picks	.... **225**

Introduction

SPIRITUAL CANCER

Today is the day of your annual check-up. You're feeling fine; you have no unusual symptoms; this year's test will be like all the others—or so you think. Your physical body appears normal, feels normal. You leave the doctor's office without giving it another thought.

Two days later you receive a phone call. Your bloodwork came back abnormal. You're asked to come back for more testing. The doctor now wants to dive deeper and you are sent for an MRI. You start to feel nervous and concerned. Another few days go by as you anxiously wait for the results. Finally, your doctor's office calls to schedule an appointment. You drive there almost on autopilot because your mind starts reeling with questions and thinking about the 'what ifs'.

And then you hear the words: "You have cancer." They found a tumor, and the tumor is malignant. It could be stage 1 or 2. It could be stage 3, or even stage 4. Your heart races; your mind follows. Thoughts run wild as those dreadful emotions immediately take root. Sadness. Anger. Resentment. Fear. They all hit you like a tidal wave. Your life is about to change dramatically and may even be over sooner than you expected. You think about your family and friends. How will they cope? As your doctor discusses surgery, radiation and chemo, you think to yourself, "How will I cope?" You have so many questions and the fear of the unknown is paralyzing. Then you reluctantly settle into a place of acceptance. You have no other choice. In an instant, your life has been turned upside down and you are forced to examine it from an entirely new and uncertain perspective.

Now how would you feel if I told you I knew a cure for your cancer? A cure that would completely heal you. A cure that goes beyond doctors and modern medicine. A cure that is 100 percent effective. More than that, it's instantaneous! Any and all cancer within your body would be eradicated. You probably wouldn't believe me at first, but you'd want to, and, eventually, I would be able to convince you. So now how would you feel? What a huge relief and the best gift ever, right? Emotionally, you would go from complete despair to immediate hope. A second chance at life!

You'd ask me what the process would be, and perhaps, the cost. What if I told you I would offer you this cure for free? That's right, free. Think of all the money I could potentially make, knowing this cure. News about me and my cure would go viral. I would be an overnight success and a millionaire or even a billionaire. I could easily become the richest, most popular person in the world. But instead, I'd offer this cure for free and I know people from all over the world would be blowing up my phone and banging down my door, just to save themselves or their loved ones from this dreadful disease.

Just imagine for a moment that I decided to keep this miracle cure to myself. That's right—I selfishly decide not to offer this cure to you or anyone, including a desperate mother and father whose child has been battling leukemia for years. As parents, there is nothing worse than seeing your child suffer and go through the worst pain and treatments possible. These parents beg and plead with me as tears of desperation pour down their faces. Of course, any normal human being with even half a heart would offer them this cure. How cold, uncaring, callous and downright mean would a person have to be to refuse this child, or anyone for that matter, this miracle cure?

But still I say, "Nope, sorry, I'm not going to share this cure with you." Can you even imagine me saying that? It makes me cringe just thinking about it. Now, what would you think of me? Sure, I'd still be a very well-known person throughout the world, however it would now be for extremely negative reasons. I'd be known as a horrible person, allowing people to suffer and die from cancer when I could cure it. How awful!

Of course, I would never be that person. I would want to share this miracle cure with the entire world! And that is exactly why I have written this book. I obviously don't have the cure for physical cancer, but I do know the cure for something far worse. Would you even believe me if I told you there was a disease worse than cancer? One that affects (and infects) every person in this world?

Statistics say that approximately forty-percent of men and women will likely be diagnosed with some form of cancer in their lifetime. But I can tell you that 100 percent of people, that's right, the entire human race, is born with and living with a fatal disease that literally goes undiagnosed. Not one of us is exempt and if not cured, it could have devastating eternal consequences. I'm talking about *Spiritual Cancer*. And for this, I do know the cure—a cure that will dramatically change your life, making it far better than you could have ever imagined. And it is my life's mission and passion to share this cure with as many people as possible.

Chapter 1

SPIRITUAL CANCER: THE DISEASE

Allow me to start by defining each word:

Spir·it·u·al, *adjective*
1. Relating to or affecting the human spirit or soul as opposed to material or physical things.

Can·cer, *noun*
1. The disease caused by an uncontrolled division of abnormal cells in a part of the body.
2. A practice or phenomenon perceived to be evil or destructive and hard to contain or eradicate.

What if I was to tell you that the simple definition for *Spiritual Cancer* is a small, ugly little three-letter word called 'sin'? The word sin makes your skin crawl, doesn't it? If Jimmy Fallon were to take a poll on the streets of New York City for the *Tonight Show* and ask people if they were sinners, I can almost guarantee they would not only be perplexed by the question, but unequivocally answer NO. Except for maybe the random Christian they happened to ask, and even then, some might still say NO.

In modern times, the concept of sin is quite complex and has become entangled in legalistic and religious arguments over right and wrong, or it is evaluated in terms of the breaking of divine law.

Now I know the last thing you want to hear is me or anyone else, preaching about religion. So, trust me, this book is not about religion because to be honest, I'm not a big fan of religion myself. I was raised Catholic and when I was a little girl, my mother would tell me she'd know if I were lying because God would turn my tongue black. So, every time I wanted to lie, I would run to the bathroom, look in the mirror, and stick out my tongue. When I saw it wasn't black, I'd run back and tell my lie. I'd then quickly check again in a mirror after I told a lie, just to make sure my tongue still hadn't turned black.

The word sin has always had a hugely negative connotation. All I remember hearing in church every Sunday was how mad God was going to be with me if I sinned or did anything wrong. Then to rid myself of these sins, I was told I had to confess my wrong doings to a priest in a confessional booth. The priest would then tell me to say a few *Hail Mary*'s combined with *The Lord's Prayer*, and then my slate was supposedly wiped clean. I guess the point of this was to fear doing anything wrong or bad. And for those who did, they were riddled with guilt for their bad deeds until they confessed them to a priest.

As years went on, I cast that religiosity to the curb and was convinced I was a good person. After all, I did good things. I've brought meals to sick friends, visited people in the hospital, I've helped the elderly and I've donated time and money to charities. I feel sympathy for the less fortunate; I've helped my friends and family when needed. I even went to church on Easter and Christmas. Sound familiar? I bet you're a good person too.

Admitting we are sinful is not only a tough pill to swallow but sounds completely ridiculous and out of date in this day and age. Overall, I think I'm a good person and I try to do the right thing. I've never killed anyone or robbed a bank. I've never intentionally hurt anyone. I guess I've told a fair share of little white lies now and then, but doesn't everyone? Don't we all think we're good people? Especially when we compare ourselves to the really bad people like Charles Manson, Jeffrey Dahmer, and Hitler. These guys were downright evil, right? We're nothing like those people.

Well, I am writing this today to shed some light on a topic. A serious problem that most of us are unaware of. It's only when we are educated and learn about something, that we can fully understand and accept it as truth.

We all know of a friend or loved one who has been diagnosed with, passed away from, or is currently undergoing treatments for physical cancer. *Spiritual Cancer* (aka: sin), like physical cancer, flies under the radar. It takes root in our hearts and spreads within us, rendering us spiritually and morally weak. It infects and affects every part of our being: our minds, our bodies, our spirits, our emotions, motives, relationships—everything. And people go about their lives without realizing, accepting, or even recognizing it. It goes completely undiagnosed.

So what exactly is *Spiritual Cancer* (sin)? How is it so easily missed? Well, let me ask you a few simple questions. Have you ever:

- Been jealous of anyone? A friend? A co-worker? A celebrity?
- Had road rage?
- Lashed out in anger toward a friend, stranger, parent, spouse, perhaps your child?
- Held a grudge toward someone who wronged you?
- Gossiped, criticized or passed judgment on someone?
- Been boastful or prideful?
- Passive aggressive?
- Told a lie, even a small little white lie?
- Been disrespectful toward others?
- Felt insecure or compared yourself to someone else?
- Made a bad or selfish decision and hurt yourself or someone else in the process?
- Been worried or stressed about a current situation?
- Thought of yourself as better than others?
- Been resentful or felt guilty about something from your past?
- Held a good old pity-party and felt sorry for yourself?
- Been bitter or ever complained?
- Felt desperate or hopeless? Suicidal?

If you happened to answer *NO* to all the above questions, go ahead and close the book and give yourself a big pat on the back because guess what? You're perfect! Otherwise, if you're truly honest with yourself, I bet you answered yes to at least one if not all of these questions. I personally fall into the 'all' category. And if you too are being honest, you must continue reading.

Sometimes we are unaware of the early warning signs of sin, just as we are cancer. But just think about the way you feel when you are jealous of someone, or resentful, or angry. If you're still holding a grudge, or you are constantly worried or fearful about your future it does not feel good. It's that sick feeling we get, or that nervous anxiety that eats away at us. And these ugly feelings slowly chip away at us, sometimes causing physical repercussions such as hair loss, stomach ulcers, or even a severe illness.

We've all woken up with a sore throat that then leads to a cold or the occasional fever that then leads to the flu. We all know the under-the-weather feeling that precedes the illness. The same exact thing happens to each and every one of us when we are infected with *Spiritual Cancer* (sin). Just as bacteria and viruses attack our bodies, sin assaults our spirits—affecting us emotionally, spiritually and mentally. I do not share this with you to alarm you, but to merely shed some light on a subject that unknowingly and subtly plagues people every day.

You may think these negative feelings and emotions are just a normal part of being human. But the truth is, they're not. We are all familiar with the term 'knowledge is power', and once you understand, recognize and come to terms with what I'm about to share with you, it is then and only then that you will be one step closer to the cure.

Chapter 2

BORN THIS **WAY**

There is a gate at the back entrance of my neighborhood. This gate will open on its own if you pull up to it close enough in your car. If you do not live in our neighborhood and aren't familiar with it though, you obviously wouldn't know this. One afternoon, I was driving my daughter, ParisElla, who was thirteen years old at the time, to soccer practice and we were running late. We idled behind a landscaping truck for what seemed like five minutes (it was probably more like five seconds) at that gate. I began to honk profusely at the driver. Then, realizing his truck wasn't close enough to trigger the gate to open, I threw my car in reverse and quickly maneuvered around him. Glaring at the driver as I sped by, I was able to position my car close enough to the gate so that it opened. The entire time I was grumbling to my daughter and telling her what a jerk that driver was.

ParisElla quickly responded, "Mom, that doesn't even make sense. That guy isn't a jerk. He just doesn't know any better." I sat in silence as she continued, "How is he supposed to know that if he pulled closer to the gate that it would open? That doesn't make him a jerk, Mom."

Her wise words stopped me in my tracks. She was right. The truck driver had done nothing wrong. However, I had. I had sinned. I know this isn't what most people would consider a 'sin' but in other words, I acted out in a less-than-perfect manner. I sat speechless for a couple of seconds and processed her simple yet profound statement. Then I said, "Honey, I am so sorry. You are so right; do you see how easily we can sin without even realizing?" I then thanked her for pointing this out to me and said, "Whatever you do, don't be like me when you grow up." We both laughed. Talk about setting a not-so-great example for my daughter that day and feeling like a mean, angry person. She sure does keep me in check! But that's the thing about sin, it's a sneaky little devil that easily goes unnoticed.

The central problem lies with our feelings of entitlement and the entitlement of society today. We instinctively feel like our actions and thoughts are justified and are so much better compared to everyone else's. We then try to convince others around us of this as well. Too many people feel that the old moral standards are useless and out of date, and we all should be free to make up our own minds about what is right and what is wrong. It's as if there is no such thing as right or wrong anymore, and we live in an 'anything goes' society where we should be free to decide how we want to live and act based on our feelings.

When we hear that ugly word 'sin', we most likely think of violations of the Ten Commandments. And then, we tend to think of murder and theft as major sins while sins of lying and cheating are judged as minor.

If we were to look at Google's definition of sin: Sin (noun), is an immoral act considered to be a transgression against divine law. This definition has some truth to it but still falls short. The biggest problem with the word 'sin' is that not many of us really know or understand the true definition of the word.

Let's first discuss sin in the most basic of terms: If you don't understand geometry and you're failing the class, how would you feel if the teacher called on you to solve a geometry problem in front of the entire class? You wouldn't feel very comfortable or confident, would you? Well, that is what happens today with people at the mere mention of the word sin. No one really understands the true meaning of sin, so just hearing the word makes us all quite uncomfortable.

So now let's expand on Google's definition. Sin is not just a "breaking of divine law," but a state that we're born into. All we need to do is replace the word 'sin' with 'imperfect'. It's just semantics and we are all born this way. That's right, the entire human race is infected with this *Spiritual Cancer* (sin) —because we all will screw up from time to time and we all will make mistakes. As the saying goes, 'nobody's perfect', which goes to show that this *Spiritual Cancer* (sin), or imperfection, is a condition we are all born with.

But our instinct is to put our defenses up, dig our heels in, and flat out deny that we are sinful. Funnily enough, it's actually a sin to deny we are sinful. Whenever we think we are good, especially when we compare ourselves to others, or have an overly inflated opinion of ourselves, it's a sin!

A scripture verse in Genesis 8:21 tells us, "…every inclination of the human heart is evil from childhood." Now before you get offended by the word 'evil', let me explain. I think we can all agree that good behavior needs to be taught, while an inclination toward bad behavior is something we are born with. This may be a tough pill to swallow but overall, human nature is corrupt, and humans are born with original sin. Sin is not only the big stuff such as murder or stealing, but as I mentioned previously, it is also the smaller, sometimes hidden, yucky things such as anger, pride, jealousy, selfishness, worry and fear.

So how is it that we are born with this sin? How could a newborn baby be born sinful? A sweet, innocent, little baby? Most people would completely disagree that a baby is born sinful. But understand that each individual who is born of this earth will also someday die, and death—both physical and spiritual—is the result of sin. Death only comes upon those who have sinned. And since infants at some point in their lives will die, they too are sinners by default. A scripture verse in Psalm 51:5 tells us, "For I was born a sinner--yes, from the moment my mother conceived me." It is a state we are born into; it is common to all of us from the moment of our conception.

And the proof is quite obvious. When keeping in mind that sin is just another way of saying we are imperfect; any mother or father can admit, the evidence speaks for itself when we think of a child's temper tantrums. Are children taught to have temper tantrums? Are they taught to shout "I want, I want, I want!" To shout, "That's mine!" Are they taught to take toys from other kids? Of course not! These are all instinctive negative (sinful) behaviors. And as our children get older, do we teach them to bully other kids or teach them to say and do mean things? Again, of course not. However, on the contrary, good behavior is learned behavior and must be taught.

As parents, we all know we must teach our children to be polite and have good manners. We teach our children to share with others, to say please and thank you, to be kind to others, to respect others and most importantly, we must teach them they cannot always get their way. Good behavior is learned behavior and it is every parent's duty to pass this on to our children. Understanding we are born imperfect (sinful) allows us to take another step closer to the cure.

You don't have to be a rocket scientist to see that the world we are living in is also imperfect. War, famine, disease, corruption, poverty, crime, despair, as well as the racial injustice and inequality we are surrounded by, are all the byproducts of this *Spiritual Cancer* (sin) I am referring to. To see George Floyd's life sadly and tragically taken from him was downright evil and sickening. The world is on fire with disease, hate, anger and violence and this must change!

It's hard to watch the news some days and be reminded of what a sad and depressing world we live in. Many of us have been living with fear after incidences like 9-11, school shootings and suicide bombings. Everyone's stress and anxiety levels are at an all-time high. How much easier would life be for us if all we did was focus on our own individual lives, our own circle of friends, and our own families? How easy would it be if we could escape and find refuge within our safe little bubbles? Yet sometimes our safe little bubbles that we try to create aren't so safe after all.

And now, not only are we entangled in this web of racial injustice, but simultaneously, we are in the midst of huge uncertainty with this COVID-19 pandemic which came out of nowhere and has blindsided us. The entire world has come to a screeching halt. Schools have closed, as have many businesses, restaurants, churches, beaches and parks. Sporting events, concerts and movie/television filming have all stopped. The global economy has crashed. Millions of people have either lost or have been laid-off from their jobs. We are now told to stay home in order to help stop the spread and to stay safe. And if we must go out, we are to wear masks and gloves and we must practice social distancing. Life as we knew it, just weeks ago, is now over.

The entire world has been affected, infected or both. Every morning I wake up, it breaks my heart to see the continued increase of new cases and deaths around the world—all because of a microscopic virus. One which started with just a few people in Wuhan, China and has rapidly spread globally. So much love, appreciation and gratitude go out to all the heroes on the frontline fighting this virus: All doctors, nurses, healthcare workers, scientists, first-responders, supermarket and convenience store employees, drivers, farmers, volunteers, etc. But even these heroes on the frontline are risking their lives as they selflessly put themselves in harm's way in order to help save the lives of others.

Nothing like this, to this magnitude, has happened to our country, or to our world, in decades, if ever. We are not only at war with an unseen viral enemy, but we are also at war with this unseen *Spiritual Cancer* which is the root cause of all this the hate and anger, as the racial tension and social unrest continues to escalate. My heart continues to break for the homicide victims, their families as well as the one's caught in the crossfire of this violence. These are cataclysmic events that have changed the world forever. Humanity is in desperate need of HELP.

The future now is scary and uncertain. It's no surprise that people are living on anti-depressants and all sorts of medications now, more than ever, to help them cope with day-to-day life. Not to say anti-depressants are a bad thing, because they're not. I'm merely pointing out that many of us need some form of help to get us through these crazy, ever-changing and sometimes scary circumstances that hit us.

Unhappiness, fear, anxiety and uncertainty are forcing us to search for that feel-good feeling or that quick fix. And because of this, there is another scary pandemic we are also at war with—global substance abuse. One of the largest concerns today is the use of opioids and according to *The National Institute on Drug Abuse*, drug use today is at an all-time high. More than 130 people in the United States die every day after overdosing on opioids. The misuse of and addiction to opioids, including prescription pain relievers, heroin, and synthetic opioids such as fentanyl, is a serious national crisis.

I just read about a man's son who passed away from a drug overdose. His son was not addicted to drugs and he wasn't in a bad mental place. He had just turned 19 and he did what many of us have done before. He went to a concert with some friends and they all took Oxy to amplify the fun. Except this time was different. Little did he know, the pill he took was laced with fentanyl.

Cheap to make and easy to mix with anything—fentanyl is ninety times stronger than morphine and fifty times stronger than heroin and if you add a few beers, it will magnify the effect even more, causing a person to fall asleep, their breathing to slow and their heart to crawl to a stop. Four other teens also died within a twenty-four-hour period that same night. This is beyond heartbreaking and tragic. It is so difficult to know who and what can be trusted, and I pray that all kids, teens and adults have the utmost discernment before taking any synthetic drugs or pills—because you just never know.

Life can be difficult and feel like a constant struggle. It's that overwhelming feeling that takes over and we feel like we're spiraling out of control. As if we're riding an emotional rollercoaster and we just want to get off. It's that feeling of despair when we never feel completely satisfied, content, or confident and we look to alternative methods to mask or numb these negative feelings.

Then there are some of us who are constantly striving to attain something bigger and better—searching for something more. If only I can make this amount of money, I'd be happy. If only I drove this fancy car, if only I lived in a bigger house. And if we do attain these things, we are still not fully satisfied.

There's a perfect line in the movie *Aladdin* where Will Smith, as the Genie, sums it up perfectly as he warns Aladdin not to wish for money and power like others do, because, as he says, "There ain't enough money and power on earth for anyone to be satisfied."

But still we are wanting more and more. Today, life is all about comparing ourselves with others and 'keeping up with the Joneses'. Designer shoes, handbags, and dresses; big homes; fancy cars—the list goes on. We dress to impress and try to look a certain way based on what we see and compare ourselves to on social media. How many 'likes' and 'followers' are we getting on social media? Men and women alike go to school, work, or post photos on social media and it's all a big competition. It's never ending.

We've seen and heard about countless stories of celebrities, actors, singers and millionaires who outwardly had it all. The ones we wish we could be! But inwardly, they were not happy. One's that ended up in jail, others who died from a drug overdose, and those who committed suicide. Something in their supposedly 'perfect' lives was missing. Something so bad, a feeling so empty, that it sadly and tragically cost them their lives—whether it was voluntary or involuntary.

A friend of mine shared her concern about her 14-year-old son's addiction to liquid marijuana. She said she and her husband have had countless discussions with him about it and his bold, unwavering response continues to be, "Well, everyone is doing it." A lot of his friends are doing it and even more kids at his school are vaping—the newest epidemic that is hitting hard with our children. Odorless, and offered in a variety of tempting flavors, these companies seem to be marketing directly to our children, for pure greed, without any care whatsoever of the harm it is causing. My friend and her husband are up against a nasty, seemingly unbeatable giant.

They have explained to him the harmful side effects of the addiction, taken his phone away, threatened him, punished him, restricted him, and have done everything in their power to encourage him to stop. And still, he continues. There appears to be nothing at this point that they or anyone can do to make him stop. Now his grades are suffering, his sports are suffering, and he doesn't even care. What has happened? Just because his peers are doing it, it is now ok. It's that quick-fix, temporary feel-good feeling. Is this the new normal? How could any of this be okay especially with the devastating long-term physical and psychological risks involved?

Robert H. Shmerling, MD, Faculty Editor at *Harvard Health Publishing* cited that the rising popularity of vaping has been dramatic, especially among teenagers. According to a recent study, about 37% of high school seniors reported vaping in 2018, up from 28% the year before. An estimated 3.6 million middle school and high school students reported using e-cigarettes in 2018; that number jumped to 5.4 million in 2019. Certainly, age restrictions (it's illegal to sell e-cigarettes to anyone under 21 (18 or 19 in some states)) aren't preventing use among teens and young adults. And nearly one out of 20 adults, 18 or older, are using e-cigarettes, according to a *Reuters* report in 2018.

Michael Joseph Blaha, M.D., M.P.H., cited on the Johns Hopkins Medicine website that among youth, e-cigarettes are more popular than any traditional tobacco product. The U.S. surgeon general reported that e-cigarette use among high school students had increased by 900 percent, and 40 percent of young e-cigarette users had never smoked regular tobacco. "What I find most concerning about the rise of vaping is that people who would've never smoked otherwise, especially youth, are taking up the habit," says Blaha. "It's one thing if you convert from cigarette smoking to vaping. It's quite another thing to start up nicotine use with vaping. And, it often leads to using traditional tobacco products down the road."

There have been news reports of lung problems linked to vaping that have resulted in many deaths. According to the CDC (as of Feb. 18, 2020) 2,807 e-cigarette users have developed severe lung disease in 50 states which has led to 68 deaths. And the numbers keep rising and most cases were among teens and young adults.

We did a great job at passing laws to prohibit cigarette smoking in most restaurants in order to protect the non-smokers from inhaling the second-hand smoke. Now these same companies have weaseled their way around the issue and created an odorless option that could potentially be even more dangerous. All for the love of money; at the risk of a person's or child's health.

We've all heard the famous saying from the Bible that warns "The love of money is the root of all evil" (1 Timothy 6:10). How true! If you think about negative emotions such as anger, jealousy and stress —nine times out of ten, you can trace the root of these negative emotions back to money, or the lack thereof. Many of us feel overworked and underpaid. How many marriages fall apart because of it? How much stress is caused by the lack of it? How much jealousy or corruption does it cause? If we were to get real with it, it sure seems like money is controlling us instead of us controlling it.

I myself know this first-hand and can only say this because I was there. For most of my life, money was a big factor controlling me. I truly believed it was the end all, be all. Nothing else mattered to me than being successful and making more and more money. My money-making skills began at the age of ten when I would mow my neighbor's lawns for ten dollars a pop. I was the richest ten-year-old on the block.

I associated money with happiness at a very young age. Ironically, the more I'd make, the more I wanted. My love of money turned me into the ultimate control freak, and it became my obsession. I believed I had control over everything. Yet looking back on the last 25 plus years of my life, I had no stability. I was constantly pursuing one goal after another, one money-making idea after another, one relationship after another, one pleasure after another. Enough was never enough and I was never truly satisfied.

Financial issues, amongst other things, take a huge toll on marriages. The divorce rate in America today is at an all-time high: 50 percent. Half of all marriages these days will fail. It's far too easy for couples to file for divorce and dissolve their marriages. No one seems to take 'till death do us part' seriously anymore. And believe me when I tell you, I am not passing judgment here. I'm twice guilty. I used to joke and refer to my first marriage as a 'mulligan', as I easily brushed it off after only eight months. With my second husband, I thought I was marrying a nerdy, bookworm-type guy who clearly appeared most trustworthy. That is, until I discovered his extracurricular habit of sleeping with other women. So back to court I went.

I have had several friends who divorced their spouses, though, just because they simply fell out of love with the person. "We were more like friends than lovers," they said. Correct me if I'm wrong but isn't your spouse supposed to be your best friend? The passionate sex may fizzle, but it's the solid communication and friendship within your marriage that will last—and grow stronger—if you put the time and effort into it.

One of the greatest threats to marriage and to love, is another hidden form of *Spiritual Cancer* (sin) called selfishness. When a wife or husband is only concerned with their own individual needs, wants, and desires, then conflict is sure to set in. I've attended many weddings where scripture from the Bible, is read. The well-known verses of 1 Corinthians 13:4-7, "Love is patient, love is kind. It does not envy, it does not boast, it is not proud. It does not dishonor others, it is not self-seeking, it is not easily angered, it keeps no record of wrongs. Love does not delight in evil but rejoices with the truth. It always protects, always trusts, always hopes, always perseveres."

But quite honestly, who really pays attention to and implements the words of this passage in their marriages and in their lives? Words are useless unless you put them into action. But because of our sinful natures, we are constantly going astray, and our selfish tendencies and pride take over with the constant need to be right and prove our spouse wrong in any and all arguments. Not to mention all the constant temptations that bombard us daily: pornography, adultery, and even just our lustful thoughts.

Adultery was never part of the equation; divorce was never part of the equation. Then entered sin. Sexual misconduct is becoming more and more prevalent. How many more celebrities, priests, producers, newscasters, doctors, etc. will be accused of and/or fired for inappropriate sexual behavior? We seem to be living in a world where immorality and lawlessness is on the rise—where people actually think they can get away with it or they think they are above the law. How did this breakdown in moral behavior even happen?

It happens because of the widespread, hidden disease of *Spiritual Cancer* coursing through our veins—and it is spreading like wildfire because we are completely unaware of it. Like this Coronavirus, which went unnoticed and unrecognized for some time. It was only when the physical signs and symptoms started to surface, and we heard reports of people sadly losing their lives, that the entire world's ears perked up—then we were all aware of it. Look how rapidly it has spread, infecting and affecting the entire world. But once the awareness and severity of this invisible enemy surfaced, it was only then that we were able to implement precise measures in order to slow/stop the spread, while scientists and doctors work tirelessly to find a way to eradicate it.

Spiritual Cancer is no different, as we are all unknowingly living and walking around with the obvious symptoms. And that is why I have written this book. To bring it to light. To expose it for the ugly problem that it is. To educate and explain how to recognize and define these symptoms. And to follow it up with the good news—there is hope and a cure. Not only hope for a better future, but also the end-all, be-all cure for this hidden, debilitating disease of *Spiritual Cancer*.

One of my daughter's favorite movies is *The Hunger Games*. In this movie, someone asks the evil President Snow why he must have a winner from the battle, instead of just executing all 24 players in order to intimidate the districts each player is representing. "Because of hope," President Snow answers. "Hope is the only thing stronger than fear. A little hope is effective. A lot of hope is dangerous." I'm going to tweak that statement by saying hope is dangerous in the best way. Perhaps the greatest psychological, spiritual and medical need that all people have is the need for hope.

A famous cardiologist named Dr. McNair Wilson remarked in his autobiography, *Doctor's Progress*, "Hope is the medicine I use more than any other—hope can cure nearly anything." Dr. Harold Wolff, a professor of medicine at *Cornell University Medical College* and associate professor of psychiatry once said, "Hope, life, faith and purpose in life is medicinal. This is not a statement of belief, but a conclusion proved by meticulously controlled scientific experiment." Wow! Who would have known or thought that hope could be scientifically proven?

Holocaust survivor Magna Mozes Herzberger was asked in a January 2017 *Atlanta Journal-Constitution* article, what helped her survive. Her response:

> "Another one of the roots of my survival was my deep faith in the Almighty. I grew up in the Orthodox Jewish religion and my whole family was religious, and ever since I was a young child, my parents instilled in me my faith in God. My trust in God in the camps gave me hope, and somehow miraculously, I survived. I was taught to have love in my heart and respect in life and to be kind and to be forgiving, and at age 18, I had all of these beautiful principles and I was in a place where it was nonexistent. But in the camps, I knew they were not going to demoralize me, and not take away my

identity. And despite everything that happened to me, I have love in my heart."

When hope dies, despair overwhelms. Hope is both biologically and psychologically vital. Hope is a feeling of expectation and a desire for a certain thing to happen. Hope is powerful, and it can easily become contagious. But amid all the unsettling circumstance of this imperfect world—there still is and always has been, a glimmer of hope. And I think we can all agree that there must be a source of this hope. So where does hope come from? Does it come from other people, our parents, our spouses, our friends, ourselves?

I once read a blog post written by an atheist. In their blog they talked about finding hope in a time of need and how a lack of faith made them feel powerless. And as I read on, they actually admitted that in a time of crisis or the loss of a loved one, they would still say a prayer, just in case. But in the normal, everyday moments, they would hone their skills on finding hope in themselves or hope in their friends, family or peers.

Call me crazy, but how can we find hope in ourselves or in others when we're all (in one form or another) blazing hot messes? Since the entire human race is imperfect, wouldn't that be the blind leading the blind? Sure, we can always turn to our family or friends for advice, encouragement, a pep talk, or simply to vent, but as imperfect humans, they too may let us down. And chances are, the advice they give will be just a temporary fix. Because the truth is, no other human being can offer us the one thing we all need—a cure. Could it be that each of us is preprogrammed to seek out something or someone greater than ourselves? Let's dive a little deeper.

Chapter 3

NEW AGE, PSYCHICS AND RELIGION

Although I shunned organized religion, I have had a belief that some greater power had to exist out there. I just didn't know what or who that was exactly. But if there was a god, I believed, like looking at a map of roads and highways, there were many different pathways leading to this so-called god. The world is filled with such thinking: It's known as the New Age Movement. New Age is the perfect have-it-your-way belief system, which is why I personally accepted this belief for many years and why it has such modern appeal.

The New Age belief system is open-minded and allows for worship of almost anything, and equates people, animals, and nature as equals. The focal point of New Age thought is to do whatever feels good, as long as you are not hurting anyone else. They accept the notion of moral relativism (situational ethics) and pluralism (universal tolerance). New Age is a compilation of the metaphysical and Eastern-influenced religions and thought systems including Buddhism, Pantheism, Hinduism, etc. The core teaching with these religions is that people are essentially good and even divine. New Age doctrine says that humans are currently estranged from god due to a lack of insight concerning god's real nature and reality.

In New Age understanding, humans are central. Humans are considered to be divine, as co-creators, and as the ultimate hope for the future of the world. These thought systems unite theology, nature, and philosophy. They believe we are all in harmony or union with each other and nature and are drawn to a god who wouldn't condemn anyone, who is impersonal, omni-present, and benevolent. An impersonal god will not reveal himself, nor will he have specific requirements as to morality, belief, and behavior. This is why New Age beliefs hold to no afterlife and why reincarnation is so appealing to them. With it, there is no judgment—there is a second chance, a third chance, a fourth, etc., until we get it right.

There is one small problem with this thinking however, because we will never get it right. We are human, and as I mentioned previously, we are imperfect and flawed. Getting it right means we have attained perfection. Which is not possible. If it were possible, or if anyone was born perfect, why aren't there at least some people who have continued in this state and remained perfect (sinless)? If humanity is not born into sin, wouldn't we expect there to be at least some people who have beaten the odds and never sinned? The truth speaks for itself; we are all sinners by nature.

New Age practitioners also encompass some or all of the following practices using their own personal methods or with the help of psychics or mediums:

- Divination: the practice of seeking knowledge of the future or the unknown by supernatural means.
- Visualization techniques: from basic mental imagery to role playing of animals or divine creatures.
- Astral projection: training your soul to leave your body and travel around.
- Crystal usage: to purify the energy systems of your body and mind.
- Channeling spirits: so they may speak through you or guide you.
- Astrology: the study of the relative positions and movements of celestial bodies interpreted as having an influence on human affairs and the natural world.

We all have questions that we want answered. How many people seek out psychics and mediums to find these answers? I can tell you that I used to! Sometimes they would be right on with their readings and other times, way off. Consulting a psychic, either in person or by phone, is done by many for fun, or out of curiosity, or because we are searching for answers. People may discover that the information seems helpful, but it is only temporary, and they may start using the psychic to make up for their own inability to cope and make decisions. They may even start relying on the psychic as a counselor to listen to their problems.

One might want to proceed with caution when following some of these New Age practices. When one takes steps to develop some of these psychic abilities, it is possible that one could unknowingly open a door to potentially dangerous forces. Some psychics will admit that when their psychic abilities expanded, so did their frightening experiences. In fact, it is common practice for a psychic to call on benevolent protective forces or to visualize 'white light' (supposedly for protection) before practicing a psychic technique or doing a reading or spirit contact. Why would they do this? What do they think they are protecting themselves from?

By doing this, the psychic is acknowledging the existence of potentially evil or harmful spirits. I'm curious to know what law says that a 'white light' is a barrier of protection against these evil entities? And why would such a light keep out any spirits? I'm not trying to sound flippant or even invoke fear by saying any of this, instead, I just wanted to touch on the topic of evil or harmful spirits because this is a subject I will be diving deeper into in a later chapter.

The Bible says not to seek out psychics or mediums. Daniel 2:27, "No wise man, enchanter, magician or diviner can explain to the king the mystery he has asked about, but there is a God in heaven who reveals mysteries," for it is God who, "alone has all wisdom and power," and who "reveals deep and mysterious things and knows what lies hidden in darkness, though he himself is surrounded by light." (Daniel 2: 20, 22).

Most religious and holy books say basically the same thing when they describe the overall message of peace, harmony and joy but none, other than the Bible, talk about a God who was selfless and self-sacrificial. If you were to look throughout the major world religions, you'll find that Buddha, Muhammad, and Confucius all identified themselves as teachers or prophets. They may have even claimed to be a god and/or people may worship them as such.

But none have ever willingly performed such a bold and self-sacrificial act as dying a horrific death because of their love for us. Theirs is about what we can do for them. Jesus, for example, was dramatically different from the rest. Jesus not only claimed to be God, but also came to say, this is what I am going to do for you — all because of my great love for you. That is what sets Jesus apart from all the others, and that difference is sacrificial love. There is no other God found in any other religion that went to such great lengths to show His immense love for all humankind.

Unlike other teachers who focused people on their words, Jesus pointed people to Himself. He did not say, 'follow my words and you will find truth'. Rather, He said, 'follow me'. An even bolder statement found in John 14:6, "I am the way, the truth, and the life, no one comes to the Father but through me."

What proof did Jesus give for claiming to be divine? He did what ordinary people can't do. The entire New Testament describes how Jesus performed miracle after miracle. He healed the blind, the crippled, and the deaf. He even raised several people from the dead. He had power over objects. He created enough food out of thin air to feed crowds of several thousand people. He performed miracles over nature by walking on top of water and commanding a raging storm to stop while He and His disciples were being tossed about in a boat. People everywhere followed Jesus because He constantly met their needs by doing the miraculous. He was basically showing people that if they did not want to believe in Him based on what he was telling them, then they should at least believe in Him based on the miracles they were seeing. John 4:48, "Unless you people see signs and wonders," Jesus told him, "you will never believe."

Throughout the Bible, Jesus said God exists, and you're looking at Him. Though He talked about His Father in heaven, it was not from the position of separation but of very close union, one unique to all humankind. Jesus said that anyone who had seen Him had seen the Father, and anyone who believed in Him believed in the Father. He claimed attributes belonging only to God: to be able to forgive people of their sins, to free them from habits of sin, to give people a more abundant life, and to give them eternal life in heaven.

Basically, Jesus was either who He said He was, or He was a fraud. Given His radical claims, we cannot logically believe that He was just a great teacher or prophet, for He would have been teaching falsehood rather than truth. As C.S. Lewis, the famous author who was once an atheist, stated:

> "I am trying here to prevent anyone saying the really foolish thing that people often say about Him: I'm ready to accept Jesus as a great moral teacher, but I don't accept His claim to be God. That is the one thing we must not say. A man who was merely a man and said the sort of things Jesus said would not be a great moral teacher. He would either be a lunatic — on the level with the man who says he is a poached egg — or else He would be the Devil of Hell. You must make your choice. Either this man was, and is, the Son of God, or else a madman, liar or something worse. You can shut Him up for a fool, you can spit at Him and kill Him as a demon or you can fall at His feet and call Him Lord and God, but let us not come with any patronizing nonsense about His being a great human teacher. He has not left that open to us. He did not intend to. Now it seems to me obvious that He was neither a lunatic nor a fiend; and consequently, however strange or terrifying or unlikely it may seem, I have to accept the view that He was and is God."

Although New Age is generally tolerant of almost any world religion or philosophy, it is opposed to the 'narrow-mindedness' of Christianity that teaches Jesus Christ is the only way to eternal salvation. They believe that all paths lead to God. As if God already knew this belief would be widely accepted, He gives us advanced warning in Matthew 7:13-14, by saying, "You can enter God's Kingdom only through the narrow gate. The highway to hell is broad, and its gate is wide for the many who choose that way. But the gateway to life is very narrow and the road is difficult, and only a few ever find it."

However, most New Agers do believe in and hold Jesus in high regard, believing Him to be a great spiritual teacher, prophet, or guru. There are many religions which claim to believe in Jesus and His teachings but it's impossible to fully follow Jesus' teachings without accepting Him first through faith. They may have learned about Him by something they read or by something they were told, but the biggest difference is that Jesus is understood and recognized by the heart, not just by the head.

New Age beliefs also savor knowledge and seek to think of oneself as good, moral and divine. They seek to elevate themselves to godhood, which then lowers the majesty and personhood of one true God. In other words, they think the universe is far too big for just one God. The New Age movement, as well as most other religions, does support honesty, integrity, love, and peace. It just wants to do it on their own terms, without one true God. Yet there is no actual doctrine or proof to support any of this. The New Age god is impersonal and omnipresent. He, she, or it has not revealed himself, herself or itself to humans, and therefore, people are not held accountable to any notions of moral law or absolute truth.

There is no objective morality in the New Age philosophy. They have tolerance for all systems of truth, meaning and purpose. They believe in a world of pure relativism, where morality and religion are strictly relative to each person's individual notion of reality itself. They have a spiritual tolerance for any and all 'truth systems'. The term for this is harmonization. But there is a slight problem with this thinking. To say there are no moral absolutes is an absolute in and of itself, which is then self-contradictory. Also, if morality is relative, then stealing may be right sometimes, along with cheating, lying, adultery, murder, etc. Living in a world of moral relativism would not bring about a positive or promising future to any civilization.

I was born with a scientific mind and am wired to seek out truth based on facts and tangible proof; rather than rituals, superstitions, theories or speculations. Truth comes from knowledge and understanding and there must be one solid foundation from where all truth is established. This is precisely what I'll be focusing on. So what exactly is truth and where does it come from?

Chapter 4

ABSOLUTE TRUTH vs. RELATIVE TRUTH

As previously mentioned, New Age beliefs have no formidable right or wrongs which means there are no absolute truths. Rather, truth to each person is relative and based on what that person thinks and how they feel. So looking at this New Age thought process, let's compare this relative truth to absolute truth.

Take math for example. We all learned in school that 4 + 4 = 8. But what if someone disagreed with us and said, "No, 4 + 4 does not equal 8, 4 + 4 = 9." We would argue this truth all day long, trying to convince one another that each of us was right. What we know, is based on what we learned from our parents or from our teachers in school, and we certainly trusted our parents and teachers enough to believe them when they taught us 4 + 4 = 8. Just because someone else truly believes 4 + 4 = 9, doesn't mean they're right. They could believe with all their heart and mind, but it doesn't mean it's the truth. Truth is based on facts.

When someone says truth is relative, they are basically saying there is no absolute truth. Some things may appear to be true to them but not true to you. If you believe it, it is true for you. If you don't believe it, it is not true for you. When people say things like, "That's fine if God exists for you, but He doesn't exist for me," that is a perfect example of them expressing that truth is relative. The concept of 'relative truth' sounds logical, tolerant and open-minded. However, upon closer analysis, it is not open-minded at all. To say, "God might exist for you, but not for me", is to say that the other person's concept of God might be wrong. This statement subtly passes judgment.

The statement or belief that truth is relative, just isn't logical. No sane person would believe or say, "Gravity might work for you, but not for me," and then proceed to jump off a tall building believing no harm will follow.

Let's look at another scenario: Two people are in a room, standing face to face. A large sphere drops between them. The sphere is two colors: One half is blue and the other half red. Each person only sees their half of the sphere. When each is asked what color the sphere is, one person says red, while the other person says blue. They argue over its color. Based on what each person sees, one only sees red on the side where they are standing, while the other person only sees blue. Each is seeing their own truth.

Only we know that the color of the sphere is both red and blue. But from their perspectives, they cannot see that the sphere is actually both colors. So, what is the truth? Are there two truths in this example? According to the first person, the sphere is only blue. According to the second person, the sphere is only red. But the absolute truth is that the sphere is both colors. We might conclude that truth is relative to each person in this situation. But if they were to step back and see the sphere as a whole, they would surely see that it is both red and blue, and that is the truth based on facts. So this truth clearly cannot be relative.

There can only be one truth. Period. Black is black and white is white. There is no gray area when it comes to truth. There simply cannot be *many truths* or a *half-truth* or *part-truth* and there must be some baseline for truth. Otherwise what we see happening in our families, our schools, our country and in the world, will continue to grow farther and farther from the truth.

Not that long-ago divorce was unheard of, and it was very rare for men or women to cheat on their spouses. Nowadays it is becoming the norm, and we are slowly accepting this as okay. Men blame it on their genetic make-up, proclaiming, "I was born this way! I was born to look at many women—not just one!" And some women are starting to accept this. Married women, now more than ever, are also starting to have extramarital affairs. Everyone is so quick to satisfy their own needs, wants, and desires, and hence the blame game begins—"My husband or wife just isn't paying enough attention to me." Or, "We haven't been getting along lately." Or, "I'm just not attracted to him or her anymore. We've just grown apart."

We live in a world which, over the years, has become more and more politically correct and more accepting of wrongs vs. rights. We live in an extremely self-serving society, where we have accepted the notion that everyone should be free to do as they want. This sounds great in theory, but because of our sinful (imperfect) natures, we are only spiraling further and further away from the core truth.

It's a fact that we have every right to believe whatever we want to. A person can believe that the sky is purple or believe they aren't very smart or attractive, or a tennis player can believe they are the best tennis player in the world, but just because a person believes these things, doesn't mean they are true. The foundation of our beliefs should be based on tangible proof and/or facts. And that foundation is called truth.

Not that long ago, people believed the Earth was flat. Just because they believed it, didn't mean it was true. Many people don't believe in a God. Again, they are free to believe whatever they want, but it doesn't mean their belief is true. And obviously the converse is also true. We all have the freedom of choice; we all have been given free will.

I read a powerful quote from Os Guinness, a popular social critic, author of more than 30 books and a leading Christian voice on social, political and cultural issues[1], which reads as follows:

> "Skeptics and relativists who undermine the notion of truth are like the fool who is cutting off the branch on which he is sitting. Without truth, science and all human knowledge collapse into conjecture (an opinion or conclusion formed on the basis of in-complete information). Without truth, the vital profession of journalism and how we follow the events of our day and understand the signs of our times dissolve into rumor. Without truth, the worlds of politics and business melt down into rules and power games. Without truth, the pre-

cious gift of human reason and freedom becomes (more of a) license and all human relationships lose the bonding element of trust that is binding at their heart.

Postmodern thinking makes us all aware of hypocrisy but gives us no standard of truth to expose and correct it. And now with the global expansion of markets through capitalism, the global expansion of freedom through technology and travel, and the global expansion of human dysfunctions through the breakdown of the family, we are facing the greatest human rights crisis of all time and a perfect storm of evil. Both hypocrisy and evil depend on lies. Hypocrisy is a lie in deeds rather than in words. And evil always uses lies to cover its oppressions. Only with truth can we stand up to deception and manipulation. For all who hate hypocrisy, care for justice and human dignity, and are prepared to fight evil, truth is the absolute requirement.

If faith is not true, it would be false even if the whole world believed it. If our faith is true, it would be true even if the whole world were against it. So let the conviction ring out from this conference. We worship and serve the God of truth and humbly and resolutely, we seek to live as people of truth. Here we still stand, so help us God.

As evangelicals we are people of the good news, but may we also always be people of truth, worthy of the God of truth. God is true. God can be trusted in all situations. Have faith in God. Have no fear. Hold fast to truth. And may God be with us all."[2]

So now I ask, "Why all this talk about God? God who? Who even believes in God anymore?" We've taken God out of most everything. We've removed Him from our conversations, from our families, from our dining tables, from our schools, heck, we've even tried removing Him from The Pledge of Allegiance. Is it even 'One Nation under God' anymore? The mere mention of God isn't very politically correct these days and makes many people uneasy. It seems more acceptable today to casually throw in the F-bomb during a conversation than it is to mention Jesus or God during a conversation.

However, it's interesting to see how common it is for the name of Jesus Christ to be written into the script of movies, TV shows, literature and used in daily conversations as a profanity isn't it? Today, we commonly hear 'Jesus Christ' to express a negative emotional state of shock, fear anger or disgust. Can you imagine the name of Krishna evolving into a profanity in India? Or Buddha becoming the favorite curse word in Tibet? Or Allah as an obscenity in the Middle East? Of course not! There is always, as there always should be, a certain level of respect and reverence surrounding the name of God —whomever your god may be.

So why is 'Jesus Christ', or even worse, 'Jesus f'n Christ', the preferred swear word in America? Or 'God-d**n'? Of all the billions of words, names and people in the world, why His name? When looking at it from this perspective, it seems a bit disrespectful doesn't it? Especially when God Himself specifically tells us in one of His Ten Commandments, "You shall not use the Lord's name in vain." (misuse the name of the Lord your God)." If any of us had any idea the severity of using the name of Jesus Christ as a curse word, I believe we would all think twice before using it.

Like herded cattle, we all follow suit, directed by society's norm. If everyone is saying and doing it, then it must be okay. Could it be that our definition of what's okay and what's normal is a bit skewed? What is even normal these days? In my generation, and the generations before, we were raised to be courteous and respectful to our parents, teachers and elders. We were never allowed to swear, and it wasn't very often that we would hear our parents, or any adults swear.

Now, I hear adults and kids alike using swear words in every other sentence. I hear kids disrespecting their parents, adults disrespecting one another, and even high-ranking government officials are speaking disrespectfully. When is enough, enough? This epidemic of *Spiritual Cancer* is running rampant and leaving a path of destruction in its wake. We have spiraled so far from the core fundamentals of truth that we don't even know what truth is anymore. We form our opinions based on what most of society believes and accepts. We are living in a world governed by entitlement—saying and doing whatever we darn well please.

No wonder hate crimes are at an all-time high. Angry, unhappy, unsatisfied and confused people surround us every day. For this world to get back on its feet and for our lives to change for the better, it is hugely important for us all to gain knowledge of absolute truth and run far, far away from this relative truth. There is a very real battle going on right now and we must fight it with love and truth. We must be intentional in our desires to get back, for our own sake and the sake of our children and families, to the root of absolute truth and be like an astronaut floating in space who relies on a cable to keep him connected to the space station.

But how can we know for sure what the truth really is? What is the baseline from which truth was established? With all this talk about God, how is anyone able to believe in something or someone they cannot see? In the 1800's, a man named Louis Pasteur was one of the greatest pioneers of science, medicine and immunology. He was a French biologist, microbiologist and chemist renowned for discovering the principles of vaccinations, microbial fermentation and pasteurization. He was quoted as saying, "A little science takes you away from God but more of it takes you to Him." So let's look to science for the answer. Yes, science. Instead of separating God from science, could it be that science is one of the greatest and most obvious ways God reveals Himself to us?

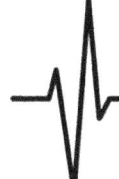

Chapter 5

IS **SCIENCE PROOF** OF **GOD?**

One hundred years ago, Albert Einstein's theory of relativity concerning space, time, and gravity sparked an explosion of knowledge. Larger telescopes were developed which enabled astronomers to look deeper into space. Then, in 1929, Edwin Hubble used telescopes to determine that the universe was not static but expanding.

Scientists are convinced that our universe began with one enormous explosion of energy and light, the Big Bang. The Big Bang Theory states that about 13.7 billion years ago all the matter in the universe was concentrated into a single tiny point, which, after one giant hot explosion, began to expand rapidly. It is still expanding today. Scientists believe this set everything in motion: the beginning of the universe, the start of space, and even the start of time itself. If you think about it, though, this theory leaves a few unanswered questions.

First, the Big Bang Theory and the scientific evidence behind it implies that space, time, and the universe had a beginning. Anything having a beginning must have a cause. So, what was that first cause? Second, the Big Bang Theory is based on the premise that the entire universe suddenly and miraculously came into existence out of nothing. How could this be? Third, according to the Big Bang Theory, in the beginning, all the matter and energy in the entire universe was compressed into an infinitesimally small point of almost infinite temperature and density. So where did this tiny little, highly explosive point or 'seed' come from? And what force held it together and then released it?

And finally, the term inflation was introduced so that the observable data would match the theory. The premise is that within the first trillionth of a second after the bang, this inflation theory caused the universe to increase in size from that supposed 'seedling' to approximately fifty percent of its current size! This idea defies all known laws of natural physics while enabling the theory to be consistent with the universe as we see it today, including how it is expanding. So what then caused this sudden expansion to happen? Objections raised about these unanswered questions are typically dismissed by stating that there must be natural laws explaining it all, yet no one has been able to discover these natural laws as of yet. The Big Bang Theory is just that. It's a theory. And the simple definition of a theory is a guess or speculation. So the Big Bang Theory is solely based on scientific speculation that many of us have just accepted throughout our lives as truth, with no definitive or absolute proof. As a science major myself, I always believed and accepted what teachers taught me. But now, I cannot help but think and wonder, who is exercising more faith in their beliefs: scientists, or those who believe in Intelligent Design? Let's take a closer look.

Agnostic and astrophysicist Robert Jastrow, said, "The seed of everything that has happened in the Universe was planted in that first instant—every star, every planet and every living creature in the Universe came into being as a result of events that were set in motion in the moment of this cosmic explosion. The Universe flashed into being, yet we cannot find out what caused that to happen." [3]

Steven Weinberg, a Nobel Laureate in physics, said that at the moment of this explosion, "The universe was about a hundred thousand million degrees centigrade . . . and the universe was just filled with light." The universe has not always existed. It had a start, but how often do we think to ourselves: what caused it? Yet to this day, scientists have no definitive explanation for the sudden explosion of light and matter.

Could it be that God was the source of this big bang? The Big Bang Theory is consistent with current measurements of the observable universe; but as you will see, it does not explain how the universe could have formed by entirely natural means. The Big Bang Theory actually requires us to accept certain premises outside the realm of the known laws of physics. The one major missing ingredient in the Big Bang Theory is the power source—a source beyond any natural physical law—a source beyond our imagination. And here in the pages of this supposed 'ancient' book called the Bible, there is a God who actually claims to be the source of the creation of the universe. In order to believe and accept the Big Bang Theory as is, you must accept certain suppositions that fall outside the laws of physics and nature. These suppositions therefore support the alternative: that perhaps our awesome universe was created by a highly intelligent Creator who must have unimaginable power.

If we were to accept the Big Bang Theory, where something formed out of nothing, all by itself, then wouldn't it be easier to imagine a universe in which conditions change unpredictably from one instant to another, or even a universe in which things pop randomly in and out of existence? There is no logical explanation for a universe that obeys rules—not just random rules, but one that abides by the rules of mathematics. This conclusion springs from the fact that the universe does not have to behave this way. The greatest scientists have been awed by how strange this is.

Richard Feynman, a Nobel Prize winner for quantum electrodynamics, said, "Why nature is mathematical is a mystery…The fact that there are rules at all is a kind of miracle." [4] Natural or biological causes are completely lacking as an explanation when programmed information is involved. If we were to take just a quick look at something more simplistic, such as a computer or computer software, we may or may not know that in order for these to function properly, they must be coded and programmed by engineering geniuses using intricate mathematical equations. Writing mathematical code to program something to work properly sounds like a mind-boggling and daunting task to most of us, right? Only a certain few, highly intelligent, highly trained and highly skilled people can handle this mathematical task.

In the early 1600's, the great Italian astronomer, physicist and engineer, Galileo was quoted as saying: "Mathematics is the language in which God has written the universe." Wow! Even for his time, that was a hugely profound statement. For those who may not know, Galileo Galilei is popularly known as the 'father of modern physics', the 'father of the scientific method', the 'father of modern medicine' and the 'father of observational astronomy'. Even by today's standards, Galileo was a highly intelligent, scientific-minded man who could very well have been onto something when he said God used mathematics to code the universe, wouldn't you agree? You cannot find instruction and precise information like this, without someone intentionally constructing it.

Could the universe and everything in it be evidence for God's existence? Let's look at some examples which suggest that God may truly exist.

First, let's consider one of the only early manuscripts that describes a God who claims to have created the universe. This would then lead us to the Bible. It is no coincidence that the Bible is listed in the *Guinness Book of World Records* for being one of the worlds' best-selling non-fiction books of all time—selling an estimated 500 billion copies. The God of the Bible is the only God who personally claims and gives details about creating the universe and all that is in it: Genesis 1:1, "In the beginning God created the heavens and the earth."

We all know that most everything we use today was created by humans. Cars, trains, planes, technology, cell phones, etc. But when was the last time you listened to the news and they announced that something just formed or popped up out of nowhere on its own? The answer is never. So wouldn't it be logical to assume since humans create things, that someone could have created the universe and all that is in it? Isn't it a little odd and perhaps a little far-fetched for us to accept that the most incredible masterpieces of all (the universe, our Earth, and our bodies) just formed, evolved or popped into existence on their own? Without any intelligent design behind them? Really?

Putting the Big Bang Theory aside, let's look at how perfectly and flawlessly the universe operates—all on its own—with supposedly no help whatsoever. Why does it? There is so much of life that may seem uncertain, but let's look at what we can count on day after day: gravity remains consistent, a hot bowl of soup left on a counter will get cold, the Earth rotates in the same 24 hours, and the speed of light doesn't change—on Earth or in galaxies far from us. How are we able to identify laws of nature that never change? Why is the universe so orderly and so reliable? Let's take it a step further and consider the following planetary wonders:

Earth

"For this is what the Lord says – he who created the heavens, he is God; he who fashioned and made the earth, he founded it; he did not create it to be empty, but formed it to be inhabited – he says, "I am the Lord, and there is no other."" (Isaiah 45:18)

The Earth's size is perfect. If the mass of Earth was any smaller, its gravity would not be strong enough to retain its atmosphere. If Earth's mass was any larger, then the pull of its gravity would be too great, and it would not be possible to have high mountains—and because there is so much water on Earth, without mountains the entire surface of Earth would be under water.

Within the interior of Earth, radioactive reactions take place that generate heat. The result is that the iron at Earth's core remains molten, and the molten iron generates a magnetic field around Earth. This magnetic field is crucial to life because it protects the Earth from damaging cosmic rays. Without the magnetic field, dangerous radiation from cosmic rays would reach Earth's surface and be harmful to life. Earth's size and corresponding gravity holds a thin layer of mostly oxygen and nitrogen gases, extending only about 50 miles above Earth's surface (roughly half the distance from New York City to the Hamptons). Earth is the only known planet equipped with an atmosphere of the exact right mixture of gases to sustain plant, animal, and human life.[5]

"You alone are the LORD. You have made the heavens, The heaven of heavens with all their host, The earth and all that is on it, The seas and all that is in them You give life to all of them." (Nehemiah 9:6)

Consider the temperature variations on Earth: roughly -100 degrees (Antarctica) to +120 degrees (Lebanon desert). If Earth were just a smidge further from the sun, plus or minus five percent, we would all freeze. If it were just a smidge closer, plus or minus five percent, we would burn up. Just a small fractional variance in Earth's position to the sun would make life on Earth impossible.

However, Earth is located at the exact perfect distance from the sun. Now get this; while Earth remains this exact perfect distance from the sun, it is rotating on its axis at a brisk 1,000 miles per hour, and then simultaneously orbiting around the sun at a speed of approximately 67,000 miles per hour! This perfect rotation of Earth on its axis allows the entire surface of Earth to be properly warmed and cooled every day.[6] Here we are moving and spinning (all at the same time) at an extremely fast rate, yet we never feel this movement. Why? Because the speed is always perfect and constant. Now, can you honestly believe that this all happens by chance? By coincidence? On its own without anyone controlling it?

It's similar to being on an airplane—on an international flight, for example—once high enough above the clouds, the plane will reach a cruising speed of 460 – 575 mph. There's a point during the flight when it doesn't even feel like the plane is moving. We can only feel the plane's movement when we experience turbulence, or when the plane slows down or speeds up. That is exactly why we cannot feel the Earth as it rotates. Although the pace at which it is rotating is incredibly fast, the movement of the Earth is so perfect that it never slows down, and it never speeds up. With all the activity going on all around us in outer space, wouldn't you think that at some point, somewhere along the line, there would be some form of interference and the Earth wouldn't be so perfect all the time? Just the absolute perfection of the Earth's rotation is enough to blow your mind isn't it?

The Sun

In the Milky Way Galaxy alone, the sun is one of about 200 billion other stars. All the other stars either produce too much or not enough ultraviolet light compared to our sun, and the planets orbiting them are not conducive to life. Is it just mere coincidence that we happen to have a sun with just the right properties to support life on Earth? If one picked a star at random, then the probability of finding one with just the right properties to sustain life on planets orbiting it would be nearly impossible.

Astronomers today are able to see billions of light years away, even though the full extent of the universe still remains unknown. Within our universe alone, there could be as many as 10 sextillion stars. The sheer size of some of these stars is mind-blowing. From our perspective, the sun is ginormous—more than one million Earths can fit inside the sun. But believe it or not, the sun is just an average size star compared to others. Scientists have found stars that are more than 1,500 times the diameter of the sun. To put it in perspective, a star of this size, if placed in the center of our solar system, would extend past the orbit of Jupiter and swallow up all the planets and their orbital space in between.[7]

"Then God said, 'Let lights appear in the sky to separate the day from the night. Let them be signs to mark the seasons, days, and years. Let these lights in the sky shine down on the earth.' And that is what happened. God made two great lights—the larger one to govern the day, and the smaller one to govern the night. He also made the stars. God set these lights in the sky to light the earth, to govern the day and night, and to separate the light from the darkness. And God saw that it was good." (Genesis 1: 14-18)

The Moon

The moon also just so happens to be the perfect size and distance from Earth for its gravitational pull. It creates tides and movement, so ocean waters do not stagnate, while simultaneously restraining our massive oceans from spilling across continents. [8]

Like the sun, the moon is critical to supporting life on Earth. The moon's gravitational pull on Earth stabilizes the tilt in Earth's axis of rotation. If this axis were not stable but varied over time, the North Pole would migrate down toward the equator, and there would be catastrophic geographical changes and climate changes on

Earth. Areas that were once fertile would become either too cold or too hot for crops to grow. As a result, life would be confined to small compact areas, and much of life would not be able to exist. In fact, without the moon, intelligent life might not exist at all. Mars has two moons, but they are too small to stabilize its rotation, and thus, Mars' axis of rotation varies widely. Our moon, however, is relatively large compared to the size of Earth, and just the exact right size to stabilize its own rotation—constantly and consistently. Amazing!

In the Bible, God Himself points out the physical evidence of His existence throughout all creation: Romans 1:20, "For ever since the world was created, people have seen the earth and sky. Through everything God made, they can clearly see His invisible qualities – His eternal power and divine nature. So they have no excuse for not knowing God."

Water

"Then God said, 'Let the waters beneath the sky flow together into one place, so dry ground may appear.' And that is what happened. God called the dry ground 'land' and the waters 'seas.' And God saw that it was good." (Genesis 1: 9-10)

It's colorless, odorless, and without taste—and no living thing can survive without it. Roughly 70 percent of the Earth is water. Plants, animals and human beings also are composed mostly of water. Roughly 70 percent of the human body is water as well. Coincidence? I'll let you decide.

Water has a wide margin between its boiling point and freezing point, which allows us to live in an environment of fluctuating temperature changes while keeping our bodies at a steady 98.6 degrees. Water is a universal solvent which means that various chemicals, minerals and nutrients can be carried throughout our bodies and into the smallest blood vessels. Water is also chemically neutral and will not affect the properties of the substances it carries. Water enables food, medicines, and minerals to be absorbed and used by the body.[9]

Water has a unique surface tension, therefore allowing water to flow upward against gravity in plant life, bringing life-giving water and nutrients to the top of even the tallest trees. Water freezes from the top down and floats, so fish can live in the winter.

Of the roughly 70 percent of the Earth's water, 97 percent comes from the saltwater in the oceans. But on our Earth, there is a remarkable system called evaporation which removes this salt from the water and then distributes that water throughout the globe. Evaporation takes the ocean waters, leaving the salt, and forms clouds that are easily moved by the wind to disperse water over the land, for vegetation, animals, and people. It is a flawless system of purification and supply that sustains life on this planet—a perfect system of recycled and reused water.[10] Could it be that this perfect system also happens by chance? Or could these facts point to a highly intelligent Creator?

"It is He who made the earth by His power, Who established the world by His wisdom; And by His understanding He has stretched out the heavens. When He utters His voice, there is a tumult of waters in the heavens, And He causes the clouds to ascend from the end of the earth; He makes lightning for the rain, And brings out the wind from His store-houses." (Jeremiah 10:12-13)

The Human Body

"Then God said, 'Let Us make man in Our image, according to Our likeness; and let them rule over the fish of the sea and over the birds of the sky and over the cattle and over all the earth, and over every creeping thing that creeps on the earth.' God created man in His own image, in the image of God He created him; male and female He created them." (Genesis 1:26-27)

The greatest of all creations is human life, our human bodies, the most magnificent of all machines—precise and efficient. All instruction, all teaching, all training comes with intent. Someone who writes an instruction manual does so with purpose.

Did you know that in every cell of our bodies there exists a very detailed instruction code, much like a miniature computer program? Back in high school, we learned that a computer program is made up of ones and zeros, that look like this: 100110101001001. The specific way each one and zero is arranged, tells the computer program what to do and for all the computer engineers out there, another term is coding.

The DNA code in each of our cells works in a very similar way. The DNA code is made up of four chemicals abbreviated as A, T, G and C which are arranged in the human cell similar to this: GTACTAAGAGCATT. Again, the way in which each letter is arranged, forms a specific code that determines a cell's behavior. Can you believe there are three billion of these letters in just ONE tiny human cell? [11]

DNA is a three-billion-lettered program instructing that one tiny cell to act in a certain way. It is a full instruction manual. And although there are several factors involved, scientists estimate that there are 37.2 trillion cells that make up the human body. So just try to wrap your brain around this; there are three billion letters in each of our body's 37.2 trillion cells. Have fun trying to figure out that number!

Just like we can program the alarm on our phones to go off at a certain time, DNA instructs each cell for its individual task. How did this programmed information end up in each human cell? These are not just chemicals. These are chemicals that instruct, in a very detailed way, exactly how the person's body should develop. Natural, biological or scientific causes are completely lacking as an explanation when highly sophisticated, programmed information is involved. It simply is not possible to find precise information and instruction like this without someone intentionally constructing it.

So now let's take a look at the dynamic framework of bone and cartilage called the skeleton. The human skeleton is flexible, with hinges and joints that were made to move. But to cut down on harmful friction, such moving parts must be lubricated. Manmade machines are lubricated only by outside sources. But the human body lubricates itself by manufacturing a jelly-like substance, called synovial fluid, in just the right amount and at every place it is needed.

The body is its own highly functioning factory, far more intricate than any factory, computer, or machine that humans have ever built. The body also changes the food we eat into living tissue. It causes the growth of flesh, blood, bones, and teeth. It repairs itself when parts are damaged and will naturally go to war to fight off foreign invaders like viruses and bacteria. The body's power source, for work and play, miraculously comes from the food we eat.

The human body also has a built-in thermostat that takes care of both our heating and cooling systems, keeping the body's temperature at a consistent 98.6°F (37°C). When we are hot, the body sends blood to the skins surface and releases drops of water in the form of perspiration, from millions of tiny sweat glands in the skin in order to keep us cool and to keep our temperature down so we don't overheat. When it's cold, the body will do just the opposite. It automatically constricts blood flow to the skin so less heat escapes and instead, blood is sent to the torso to protect and keep the vital organs warm.[12] I was a science major, and this just blows me away. It's incredible to me how this happens automatically, on its own, without us thinking about or telling our bodies to do this. It's truly amazing.

And unlike anything man-made, our body can recreate itself from just one microscopic cell from a male combined with one from a female. Our bodies have been designed with the ability to pass on to the next generation, the programmed information required to form another person.

The heart is a strong, muscular pump, that pushes blood through thousands of miles of blood vessels. Blood is the life force of all mammals and has the most important job of carrying oxygen and nutrients to every part of the body. The heart pumps an average of 1.5 gallons of blood every minute and pumps enough blood to fill more than forty, 50-gallon drums in just one day. Amazing.

Simultaneously, the brain is processing an unfathomable amount of information. Our brains take in all the colors and objects we see, the temperature around us, the pressure of our feet against the floor, the sounds we hear, the dryness of our mouths, and even the texture of our phones.

The brain holds and processes all our emotions, thoughts, and memories. All while subconsciously keeping track of the ongoing functions of our bodies—like our breathing patterns, eyelid movement, hunger, and movement of the muscles in our hands. We are not consciously telling our bodies to breathe, pump blood, blink or to move our legs when we walk. The human brain is doing this for us and processes more than a million messages a second. Our brains then measure the importance of all this data, filtering out the relatively unimportant. This screening function is what allows us to focus and operate effectively in our world. [13]

The brain functions differently than other organs. There is an intelligence to it—the ability to reason, to produce feelings, to dream and plan, to take action, and to relate to other people. The brain is the center of a highly complex computer system more wonderful than the greatest computer ever built. The body's computer system computes and sends billions of bits of information throughout the body—information that controls every action. In most computer systems, the information is carried by wires and electronic parts. In the body, our nerves act as the wires that carry the information back and forth from the central nervous system.

And in one human brain, there is probably more electrical circuitry and more wiring than in all the computer systems in the world put together. Just to give you an idea, there are approximately 225,000,000,000,000,000 (225 million billion) interactions between cell types, neurotransmitters, neuromodulators, axonal branches and dendritic spines, and that doesn't include the approximately 1 trillion glial cells which are important for neural information processing (an excerpt from "10 Important Differences Between Brains and Computers," *ScienceBlogs.com*). Because the brain is nonlinear, and because it is so much larger than all current computers, it clearly is the most complex and awe-inspiring of all.

In fact, as you are looking at and reading the pages of this book, you are actually seeing with your brain. However, the message is carried there from another amazing structure, the human eye. In the eye, the focus and aperture are adjusted automatically, similar to modern cameras, and it can distinguish among seven million colors and handle an astounding 1.5 million messages—simultaneously. [14]

The sounds we hear, are being played on a perfect little musical instrument inside our ear called the cochlea, which is rolled up and looks like a tiny seashell. Sound waves travel down the auditory canal and are carried by three small bones of the middle ear called ossicles, which are just the right shape and size and sit exactly in the right position for us to hear properly. The outer ear operates in air, but the cochlea, is filled with liquid, and transfers sound waves from air to liquid.[3] This process is one of the most baffling known to science.

The complexity and perfection of our universe, as well as our planet Earth, combined with the intricacies and sophisticated design of our bodies, seems to logically point to a deliberate, highly intelligent designer who not only created our universe, as well as everything in it, but also sustains all of it today. Could it be God Himself? Colossians 1:16 says, "For by Him all things were created, both in the heavens and on earth, visible and invisible, whether thrones or dominions or rulers or authorities—all things have been created through Him and for Him."

For those who still believe we evolved from a single-celled amoeba, it is true that the raw material—the basic chemicals in our body—can be found in the dust of the ground. However, these chemicals cannot magically arrange themselves into complex cell tissues and organs and then simultaneously operate such perfect, intricate systems. This can only happen logically with the input of extreme intelligence.

The book of Genesis teaches that God took "the dust of the ground" —basically a heap of chemicals—shaped a man, and then blew into his nostrils the breath of life: Genesis 2:7, "Then the LORD God formed man of dust from the ground, and breathed into his nostrils the breath of life; and man became a living being." Man became a living soul, different from animals. We are more than the chemicals that form our body. We are a special creation of God. We are God's masterpiece—His workmanship, the crown of His creation. We are made in His image. Call me crazy, but doesn't it seem far more logical to believe and accept that we were created by a highly intelligent Creator, rather than just by chance?

My husband goes for a run almost every day. This is the time he spends in prayer with God. He came in the front door one morning and was so excited to share something with me. He is a businessman who loves developing and implementing new systems in order to make our companies run more efficiently. He excitedly asked me, "Hun, guess what the most perfect system is?" "What?" I asked. "The Solar System," he said. I smiled, as he shared his epiphany.

He continued, "It's the only system that is solely owned and operated by our perfect God. With no human intervention. No system on earth will ever run as perfectly because all other systems are developed, operated or somehow influenced by imperfect humans." I loved this.

To think that the Earth even sits where it does in space and time is a miracle. If it were to shift any closer to the sun, we would all burn up and die. Or if it were to shift any farther away from the sun, we would all freeze to death. So what really keeps the Earth so perfectly in its place as we sit suspended in space? What causes it to rotate so perfectly each and every day with zero interference — ever? Even the greatest man-made computer will have glitches because nothing made by humans is ever perfect because we're not perfect. So why should we accept or believe answers from imperfect scientists who could potentially give imperfect scientific explanations?

If we can't control the beating of our own hearts and if a tree has no control over the height it will grow, then who does? If the seed of a tree was not already pre-programmed, there would be nothing to stop it from continually growing taller. It would continue to grow and grow, high above the Earth and into the clouds. Clearly, they are pre-programmed to stop growing at a certain height and there are hundreds of thousands of pre-programmed DNA within each tiny little seed. Sure, we can bury a seed in some dirt and water it. But do we really have control over the growth process — or control over what it is already pre-programmed to do? I think not.

Similarly, humans start from a tiny, microscopic "seed" as well, and we have no control over the tiny little fetus that develops within a woman's body. Every living thing on earth begins the same way. Who pre-programs them? We have created hundreds of thousands of inventions since the beginning of time. What inventions have humans created that hasn't needed humans to sustain it? All created things (whether living or mechanical) constantly need to be sustained. Nothing can live and function on its own — nothing.

Things break or fail. Cars, machines, computers, you name it. And whatever we have created, we have the ability to fix, right? And even our ability to fix things is sometimes limited. A doctor can perform open-heart surgery to fix a blockage, but once the blockage is fixed, who does the rest? Who heals the incisions made within the body? We do have some control, but it is limited.

Think about this; if God created the universe and sustains it perfectly, then perhaps the reason it never breaks down and never needs fixing is because it is the one thing, we as humans cannot meddle or tamper with. So, if God also created us, then isn't it logical to assume that He has the ability to fix us? I'm not just talking about fixing us in a physical sense (although He does that too), but also in a spiritual sense. And I think we can all agree, with the stress and challenges we face daily, we sure could use some help. We just need to get ourselves out of the way. Because whatever God creates, God can sustain. And He will, in His time.

Chapter 6

TIME IS MONEY

In 1748, Benjamin Franklin, one of the founding fathers of the United States, wrote in a book the popular statement, "Remember that time is money". This phrase is widely understood to mean that you must use your time wisely in order to make money. This interpretation is true, but we could also interpret this saying in a slightly different way. Let's focus on just the words 'time is money'. In other words, time is like, or equivalent to, money.

Each day, we get 24 hours of time deposited into our daily accounts. Think about it; time is one of the most valuable resources given to us and we get to decide how to 'spend' this time each day. Like our money, we get to choose how much to spend, how much to invest and how much to give away. Time, however, is more valuable than money because we can use our time to make money, but we cannot use our money to buy time. And the time deposited into our accounts is the same for all of us. Nobody will ever have any more or any less.

Steve Jobs summed it up perfectly when he said, "My favorite things in life don't cost any money. It's really clear that the most precious resource we all have is time."

Time passes quickly and each moment that passes is unique and we will never get it back. Doesn't it seem like yesterday when we were kids playing ball in the backyard with friends in our neighborhood? Or for those of us who have grown children—doesn't it seem like just yesterday when we were changing their diapers? One thing is for sure, time flies.

We live in a very dynamic, ever-changing world. Everything around us is moving. Yet one thing remains constant, and that is time. Time itself is yet another miracle surrounding us that we easily overlook. If it wasn't for time, life wouldn't be as we now know it. Time is fixed and never changing and is a perfect example of an absolute truth. It is measured in seconds, minutes, hours, days, weeks, months and years. Every second that ticks by is set and precise. There is no human that has the power to change time. Time, as we know it, is perfect. Nothing happens too fast, nor too slow.

Which leads me to the next question: Did you know that we wouldn't even exist, or in other words be 'seen' here on earth if it weren't for time? Time is perfectly set at a rate for us to function and exist. Because of time's precise movement—we are moving slow enough, yet also fast enough, allowing us to be seen and to see what is going on around us.

Let me to explain. Take a car, for example. We drive them and we see them going by us on the road. But if we were to take a video of a moving car and gradually speed it up, it would become blurry and eventually it would go so fast that we'd no longer be able to see it. And the converse is also true for slow-moving objects like grass growing and flowers blooming. Only in time-lapse movies or videos, where we speed up the movement of time, can we see these wonders happening. Not only would the speeding up of time cause most objects to no longer be visible, but the same can be said about the slowness of time as proven by the growth of grass.

For things that move too slow for the eyes to see, we've used technology and camera equipment to make time-lapse videos of a tiny seedling growing into a mature flower within seconds, or we've seen a time-lapse video of a baby that grows into an adult within minutes. Or if something happens too fast, we can play back a slow-motion video to see the smallest of details: like an instant replay of a football player catching the ball in the end zone, only to see that his foot was actually just outside the line. In a case like this, time moved too fast for the naked eye to see and we needed to slow things down in order to catch the smallest detail.

Time is a very interesting concept. Think about the speed of sound and the speed of light; light travels so fast that if humans could travel at the speed of light, we could travel to the other side of Earth in less than the time it takes to snap our fingers. Crazy, right?

Our lives also revolve around time. If I asked you for the time, I have a pretty good idea what you'd do. You'd glance at your watch or phone, check the time, and respond appropriately. If you were enjoying what you were doing at the moment, you might exclaim, "My, how time flies!" If you weren't especially happy about what you were doing, you'd probably groan, "We still have two more hours." Time has been a common excuse for many failures. We wave them away saying, "I didn't have time." Most of us check the time several times a day—or several times an hour. Sometimes we do it more often than we should. We're obsessed with time.

And just before we were hit with this COVID-19 pandemic, we were pressed for time now more than ever. Places to go, people to see, appointments to get to, driving our children here and there, traveling to and from work. We fit so much into each day that we hardly had time for ourselves. Now we have all the time in the world. Isn't it interesting how everything has come to a complete standstill? As if we are sitting within what appears to be a global 'time-out', just waiting for the world to reboot. We have all been so distracted by our crazy, busy lives, that we lost touch of what truly is important—like quality time spent with family and friends. I'm guilty as charged! But now, I can't tell you how many times we've played Monopoly, card games, family bike rides, swimming, running, working out, kicked the soccer ball around, plus the countless hours of family *Netflix* time. Laughing and creating new memories has been such a silver lining in these unusual circumstances. It has been a beautiful reminder of my own childhood—minus the cell phones and technology.

Speaking of which, I'm sure it wouldn't surprise you to know that one of the greatest robbers of time today are our cell phones. Research shows that American adults spend an average of five hours per day and teens are spending an average of seven hours per day on their phones. I admit, cell phones do play a very important and convenient role by keeping us connected to our family, friends and even our work. But we must be careful, because the social media addiction is real. Partly due to a person's fear of missing out. It's the endless posting, scrolling, liking, comments, selfies, tweeting, snapping, streaks, hashtags and the list goes on and on. Our phones have become the world's biggest distraction and addiction.

Then there are some of us who spend our time working long hours to make more and more money. And I get it; we all want better lives for ourselves and our families. But just remember, when we die, money cannot be taken with us. It's not the best idea to work so excessively, that we neglect spending that quality time with our families. A healthy balance can always be found.

Not to mention the time we spend worrying, stressing, or grinding on things we're trying to control. We must not allow circumstances, nor our phones, to control us. We must control them by mentally letting things go and realizing what truly is important. Feeding into any negative emotion is a complete waste of time and can often become crippling.

After any traumatic experience that causes us emotional pain, they tell us time is a healer. But is it? Does time really heal us? Or is it merely the passage of time that blurs the bad memories until they somewhat fade. Time itself, does not have the ability to heal our pain. It may help make our pain less over time, however it doesn't have the power to heal or cure our pain. But I'm excited to tell you what will!

The fact is, everyone goes through good times and bad times; together they make up the seasons of our lives. It is best to be thankful during the good times in our lives and thankful that the bad times won't last. If things aren't going our way, we must give it time and be careful not to let these bad times defeat us. It is wise to set our sights on the big picture, the duration of the season, rather than focus on the peaks and valleys of time.

We must be like a gymnast walking across a balance beam. Envision good things (an A on a test, a new job you were hired for, an award you just received, etc.) falling to the right and bad things (you just failed an exam, you just lost your job, someone hurt you, etc.) falling to the left. Once they've fallen, they've fallen. We may be tempted to mentally jump off either side of the beam to grab and hold onto things that have already fallen. But it is best to let them go. Incidences in life will constantly try to derail and distract us, trying to push us off that beam to one side or the other. But we must stay focused as we look ahead to the future. The key is learning to accept bad circumstances, as graciously as we accept good circumstances.

Nothing around us is stagnant. Everything is in a state of motion and movement. So with all this in mind, do we ever consider where time comes from? Or who invented it?

Time, as we know it, is a very recent phenomenon. Through the persistence of two men—Charles Dodd, a schoolteacher, and William Allen, a railroad engineer—time was standardized in the United States on November 10, 1883. It wasn't until the American railroads accepted Dodd and Allen's idea of four time zones across the United States that trains could schedule their arrivals and departures with any degree of consistency. Before that, every community decided what time it was on its own. It took another year for a meeting of 26 nations to determine the 24-hour worldwide times zones that we use today.

We didn't always have seven days in our week, either. Back in 1792, the French tried a 10-day week with 10 hours in a day, 100 minutes in an hour, and 100 seconds in a minute. But it didn't work. The Russians tried a five-day week in 1929, and even named the days of the week after colors. But nobody paid any attention, so the Russians switched to a six-day week in 1932. Finally, when they realized that still didn't work, they abandoned the whole idea and returned to the standard seven-day week.

Though the way we understand time is relatively new, God has been working with time since the beginning of creation. He's the originator of time: Genesis 1:5: "So the evening and the morning were the first day." The Bible says that God created the entire universe in six days, and on the seventh day He rested. On the seventh day, all of creation was complete. Thus, the number seven represents complete-ness. After the seventh day the world was complete, and nothing could be added to it neither could something be taken away from it without marring it. So the world was perfect on the seventh day. Time existed from the very beginning of creation and it would appear that God was the One who originally established the perfect seven-day week from the beginning.

When we consider the perfect rotation of Earth, the perfect path Earth takes around the sun, the seasons that occur at the exact same time every year, and the perfect 24-hour days that never change, we have to wonder how this is all possible? How could time be so perfect year after year all the time? The days of the month (except for the occasional February) never change.

Time is a perfectly synchronized standard that is going on all around us, second by second, minute by minute. Time is an interesting concept. It is irreversible. No one has the power to go back in time and no one has the power to move forward into time. None of us have the power to change or control it. In our everyday world, time is a constant.

And for each of us, our time spent on earth is uniquely different. We all have a specific time, day and year we were born. With that said, we also have an expiration date—a specific time, day and year when we will pass away. In a world of heroic medical care and wonder drugs, let's not forget that just as the day of our birth was part of God's eternal timetable, so is the day of our death. We cannot run from death, and we certainly cannot hide. We may be able to prolong our lives for a bit, by basically 'buying some time', but we all will eventually meet the same fate.

Time is of the essence and balance is key, so it is wise to not waste time festering or focusing too much on either. A good analogy is to envision ourselves wearing blinders, keeping our eyes and thoughts focused in the present moment as we look straight ahead to the future. There's a reason why the front windshield of our car is so much larger than the rear-view mirror. What lies ahead of us is far more important than what is already behind us.

So, it is important to be aware of how precious time is—it's a commodity. And once it's gone, we can never get it back. We must be purposeful with our time and be cognizant of the things that sap our time because when we waste time, we are only robbing ourselves. Time spent and invested in others; whether it be our children, relatives, friends or helping a stranger in a time of need is what makes the biggest impact. Time spent with people is the legacy we can all leave behind. Thomas Edison was quoted as saying, "Time is really the only capital that any human being has, and the only thing they can't afford to lose."

When the clock strikes midnight at the beginning of each new year, many of us will make New Years' resolutions. We have every intention of 'rebooting' our lives in order to make changes for the better. But we must remember that every month, every week and every day is also a new beginning. Every day and every moment is an opportunity for a new beginning. We don't have to wait for a new year to make changes in our lives. We can make them now.

So, what time is it for you? How are you using your time? What will you do during the time you have left here on earth? Are you giving of your time with others? Time is precious to all of us, and just like our money, we get to choose how to spend it—so we should spend it wisely.

Life is short. The time we have here on earth is miniscule compared to eternity. Every day is a gift we should be especially thankful for. I remember someone once saying that with every day that passes, we are another day closer to our death. I know that may sound a bit morbid, but it's true and it's something not many of us think about. Our time here is limited, and nobody likes the idea of facing death because the thought of it invokes fear. Fear of the unknown. But I'm here to tell you, it doesn't have to be this way. Once I explain the cure for this *Spiritual Cancer*, it will surely give you great peace, as well as hope.

One of the most profound realizations about time that hit me when I first started to believe in Jesus was the date and year we go by. We are currently living in the year 2020. And as I just mentioned, the entire world goes by the same twelve-month calendar each year.

Have you ever thought about where the year 2020 comes from? The year 2020 marks the number of years since Jesus' death and resurrection. We all know the Earth is older than 2020 years, but what exactly happened 2020 years ago that literally stopped and re-started time? Think about it.

Why are we living in the year 2020 if the world is actually much older? Early textbooks refer to time as BC (Before Christ) or as AD (Anno Domini-in the year of the Lord). 500 BC establishes a time as 500 years before the birth of Christ and 500 AD accounts for 500 years after the birth of Christ. Clearly Jesus had to be a pretty big deal considering the entire worlds account of time revolves around Him. Something cataclysmic had to have happened for time to literally stop, and then start again—as if the power switch to the earth was momentarily shut down when Jesus was born, then the reboot switch was turned on and the earthly clock was reset. So what are the chances that the entire world would now go by this universal time of 2020? 2020 years after the birth of Christ. Coincidence? I'll let you decide.

Chapter 7

CONTROL OR NO CONTROL? THAT IS THE QUESTION

Con·trol, *noun*
    1. The power to influence or direct people's behavior or the course of events.

Control is the idea that we can strongly influence how something will happen or how we can influence another person's actions or behavior.

Long before having a child of my own, I remember being on an airplane while a nearby passenger's toddler screamed non-stop throughout (what seemed like) the duration of the flight. Not only was this the most annoying thing to deal with, but I also thought to myself, "When I have my own kid, mine will never do that!"

My own daughter, ParisElla, was born several years later. I flew many times with her from the time she was an infant. And making sure to live up to those words, I must say, all had gone quite well as I'd board the plane with my trusty backpack which I referred to as my 'bag of tricks'. In it, included anything and everything I could think of to keep my little munchkin happy, and fully occupied throughout the duration of the flight. I totally thought I had this 'happy and content toddler thing' under control—that is, until one such flight. She had just turned two and she was still considered a lap child. We experienced an unusual amount of turbulence on this particular flight. The pilots voice came over the intercom and insisted that everyone stay seated with their seatbelts on. That included the flight attendants. Well, ParisElla, now old enough to have a mind of her own, wanted no part of this. She wasn't quite old enough for me to reason with her and explain why she needed to stay seated on my lap, yet she was surely old enough to protest and put up a fight. That was when the struggle began.

A flight attendant, noticing the wrestling match that was going on, insisted that I securely hold onto her. For crying out loud, couldn't she see I was trying? Obviously in a perfect world that would have been possible, but unfortunately being held on my lap was the last place she wanted to be. Instead, she proceeded to kick, flail, push, punch and scream at the top of her lungs for the remaining hour of the flight. The tighter I held her, the harder she fought. I had no idea a 2-year-old could have such herculean strength, combined with blood-curdling screams that belonged in a horror movie. I began to sweat profusely and she and I both had tears running down our faces. It was in that moment I realized I had zero control over this child. And I mean ZERO.

Everyone around me was staring at this lovely spectacle—and I could sense by the looks I was getting, that most were as annoyed as I had been in the past. A perfect example of 'what comes around, goes around'. I was overcome with embarrassment, frustration and anger all wrapped into one.

There was nothing I could say, do, or even offer her to make her stop. Her mind was set, and she was prepared for a long, drawn-out battle. After a good solid hour of this (which seemed more like forever!) the plane was finally landing as she slowly started to settle down, most likely due to exhaustion. As we taxied down the runway, I wiped the sweat from my brow and the tears of embarrassment and frustration from my eyes and I immediately began apologizing to the people sitting near me. Some were supportive, saying they too had experienced this with their children, while others were downright annoyed. I can't say that I blamed them.

We finally pulled up to the gate and the fasten-seat-belts light was turned off. I immediately stood up and loudly apologized to the entire plane as I jokingly mused, "Drinks are on me!" Needless to say, I am much more empathetic and understanding with crying children on planes now.

There are so many things that surround us daily that are beyond our control. As I mentioned in the previous chapter, the basic functionality of our own bodies and the height and rate at which a tree grows indicate what little-to-no control we have. As well as time, weather, the seasons, the rotation of the earth—none of these major things that are going on all around us daily are under our control.

So the question remains. Do we have control over our lives? If I was asked that question several years ago, I would have been the first to admit that I absolutely had control of my life. I was in a New Age mindset, believing I had the power to create my own destiny through the power of intention. What I could envision, I could manifest. I embraced this entire New Age concept and believed in mind over matter. If I thought and/or focused long and hard enough about something, I thought for sure it would happen.

But the true and simple answer to that question is both yes and no. What we do have control over are the choices we make. Which is our free will. But once we make our choices, we then lose control of the circumstances surrounding those choices.

Choices surround us daily—like what our plans are for the day, or what car we buy, where we drive our car, or the job we accept, the clothes we buy, or the university we go to, the vacations we take or who we date or marry. But just think for a moment about the variables surrounding even those choices that are still not in our control. You may plan to bring your child to school one day, but your child could wake up with a sore throat and fever and not be able to go. Or you could plan to drive to the store, but your car won't start. Or you could drive a mile down the road, and someone rear-ends you at a stop sign. You could have planned months in advance a family vacation, until the day your boss tells you you've been promoted to VP of the company. This certainly is amazing news, but this promotion includes relocating to another state during the time you were supposed to take that family vacation. Circumstances beyond our control surround us daily. Some good, some not so good.

So, who or what controls these circumstances? Everything I have mentioned thus far seems to point to fact that someone or something would have to be in control. These circumstances cannot be easily brushed aside as random occurrences. Think about the sheer chaos this world would be in if there was no order, no laws, or if we truly believed in random occurrences. Look at the law of gravity, for example. Just imagine how crazy and chaotic this world would be without the law of gravity! Everything, including us, would be aimlessly floating around without any control or stability whatsoever, as it is in outer space.

With that said, could it be that the same entity that created us, time, gravity, that formed and sustains our perfect universe, including earth, would also have control over all events and circumstances? The logical answer is yes. Or you could continue to believe in random occurrences—which seems to take far more blind and illogical faith to believe in than to believe in an intelligent creator. Think about this; humans have built and created cars, houses, bridges, skyscrapers, technology and so forth. As I mentioned before, how often do we hear about things miraculously popping into existence? For the most part, everything we see and use daily was created by humans. So why is it so hard to believe that someone may have created us and the world we live in? Doesn't it seem much more logical to believe this, than to believe we just spontaneously popped into existence without some form of intelligence behind it?

When we think of God as this Mighty Creator, we cannot bind His divine knowledge and power to the limitations of created human knowledge and power. God is not just another part of nature. He is not even the greatest part of nature. Rather, He is nature's author and sustainer. He is the Creator, totally separate and above and beyond the created universe. He is the superpower above all powers in every area of His creation, including the weather, as stated in Job 37:6, "He directs the snow to fall on the earth and tells the rain to pour down." And again, in Job 37: 9-12, "The stormy wind comes from its chamber, and the driving winds bring the cold. God's breath sends the ice, freezing wide expanses of water. He loads the clouds with moisture, and they flash with his lightning. The clouds churn about at his direction. They do whatever he commands throughout the earth."

Christians affirm their belief in the sovereignty of God, but even their faith is challenged in times of natural upheaval, national disaster, or personal affliction. Pain and poverty, disease and death, sorrow and suffering—all tend to cause us to think seriously about God as Creator and controller of the world. Especially as we sit in the midst of this COVID-19 pandemic which has literally turned our lives upside down with its devastating effects on the entire world. It is not always easy to believe that God is in control, but it might make more sense if I was to re-work that statement a little—changing the default line from 'God is in control' to 'God is always good'.

In other words, He is always able to bring good from any situation as we trust Him. So even if we make a seemingly bad or wrong decision, God, in His sovereignty, can make something good from it. Yes, His awe-inspiring, miraculous, all-knowing sovereignty means that while we make our choices, He can still take our weaknesses and mistakes and use them for His glory. Which means that no matter what happens to us outside of God's perfect will, we can place our trust and faith in Romans 8:28, "…And we know that God works ALL things for the good of those who love Him." ALL things means ALL —the good, the bad and the ugly.

The word 'sovereign' is a pretty awesome word. It conveys the idea of superior and supreme, primary and paramount, un-equaled, unexcelled and all-knowing. The God of the Bible is not only referred to as sovereign, but He is eternal and self-existent. He is supreme in excellence and perfect in all His ways. He is the only One who is self-contained and self-controlled, with the right and power of self-government. His capacities and capabilities far surpass the scope of human reason. In addition to being sovereign, God is Holy and righteous. This means that He can do no wrong. If God could do wrong, He would cease to be God.

Most of us have heard the story of a little shepherd boy named David who had the bold faith to take down and kill Goliath, the giant, a great enemy to his people, with a small slingshot and a stone. When David grew, he was appointed King and to this day, he is known as one of the greatest kings of all time. King David stood before his congregation and prayed aloud to God, in 1 Chronicles 29:11-12, "Yours, LORD, is the greatness and the power and the glory and the majesty and the splendor, for everything in heaven and earth is yours. Yours, LORD, is the kingdom; you are exalted as head over all. Wealth and honor come from you; you are the ruler of all things. In your hands are strength and power to exalt and give strength to all."

King David testified that affliction was a learning experience for him. He wrote in Psalm 119:71, "It was good for me to be afflicted so that I might learn your decrees." This leads to one of the most popular questions of all time—why would God allow us to suffer and allow bad things to happen? I will definitely answer this popular question in a later chapter, but as for now, we all know suffering in this lifetime is unavoidable and believe it or not, it is a required course in God's school of life, and as odd as this may sound, can be looked upon as a great lesson for each of us.

Circumstances beyond our control happen to us daily and some of the worst trials for me have actually been the most incredible blessings in disguise.

Starting with my adoption.

I was given up for adoption as an infant and was raised by a wonderful adoptive family. They provided me a good, stable household and upbringing. But I desired more: more love, more affection, more of everything. I was never satisfied or fully happy. So from a very young age I was difficult, rebellious and disrespectful. My parents who raised me were quite strict and would say 'no' a lot. It was their way of protecting me but instead of obeying them, I became more rebellious and perfected my craft of manipulating and lying in order to get my way. Whatever I' set my mind to, I'd stop at nothing to get it. In the process, I hurt a lot of people, including my parents, my friends and even myself, as a result of my bad decisions.

I did a fair amount of underage drinking, experimented with drugs, sex, got caught stealing, was arrested, you name it. I did things most wouldn't do, and I'm not proud of it. Many of my pathways led to destruction—self destruction. My teen years were painful and filled with heartache and that pain flowed right into my twenties. For years I questioned why I was even born. I contemplated suicide. I was constantly searching for something yet had no idea what I was searching for. No matter what I did, I could not satisfy that empty feeling within me.

In November 1999, my mom who had raised me passed away from her life-long battle with diabetes. It was after her funeral when my dad turned to me and asked, "Why haven't you ever looked for your birth mom?" "Because I knew it would hurt Mom's feelings," I replied. He agreed but then said he thought it would be a good idea for me to find her. A few days later he handed me a piece of paper with the name of the adoption agency. I was 29 years old at the time and as I looked down at the paper I was hit with a tidal wave of emotion. Could this be it? The moment I had been dreaming about my whole life. Seeing my biological mother's face for the first time. To look her in her eyes and instantly recognize her. To hear what her voice sounds like, to feel her arms as she wraps them around me. I was overwhelmingly excited and convinced that meeting her would finally fill that emptiness I had been trying to satisfy my whole life.

A few days later, I called the adoption agency and spoke with a lovely woman. I explained to her my situation and she asked me a few questions, one being my date of birth. She paused and then sadly told me not to get my hopes up. The agency's practice was to send a letter to the address they had on file—an address that was 30 years old. She warned me that the chances were very slim that my biological mother still lived at that same address. And if by chance she still did, then it would be the decision of my biological mother to agree to meet me or not. She said it would take her at least a couple weeks to do her due diligence and she would get back to me as soon as she heard anything.

About a week-and-a-half later, I received the phone call. The woman at the agency told me she had some really good news but also some bad news. She said it would be best for me to meet her at the agency so she could explain everything to me in person. My heart raced with nervousness and excitement with the hope of meeting the woman who gave birth to me. I longed to just hear the sound of her voice and to finally find that one source of true love I'd been searching for.

It was an icy cold day in January 2000. I drove from my home in Massachusetts, where I was living at the time, to Providence, Rhode Island. As I walked up the stairs of an old colonial house-turned-office building, the woman I had spoken with on the phone, greeted me at the door. "Oh, you look just like your mother!" she exclaimed. With a puzzled look on my face I asked if she knew my mother. "No dear, come on in and have a seat. I'll explain."

I followed her into her office and sat in a chair in front of her desk. She looked down at the papers in front of her, grabbed what looked like a newspaper and she slowly handed it to me. It was indeed that day's newspaper and she told me to look at the front page. My eyes were immediately drawn to a photo of a woman who looked strangely familiar, because she looked like me. As I quickly read the headlines, I noticed another photo of a man, her fiancé, who had just been found guilty of first-degree murder. The verdict came in and was on the front page of the newspaper the very same day I arrived at the adoption agency. "Was this my mother?" I asked. "Yes dear", the woman sadly responded.

The murder happened in September 1999, the night of my biological mother's daughter's wedding. Evidently my biological mother's fiancé was jealous of her ex-husband (my half-sister's father) who was also at the wedding, and they were arguing that day. From what I heard, they argued quite often and that night, she gave her engagement ring back to him and called off their engagement.

He was not happy about this and basically told her if he couldn't have her then nobody else would. He grabbed a large policeman's flashlight from the trunk of his car and proceeded to beat her over the head. As she fell to the ground, he heard a car coming down the street, so he jumped into the driver's seat and quickly reversed over her body and raced away, dragging her lifeless body a few feet behind him. She passed away that night.

After reading this, I began to sob uncontrollably. I had heard about this horrific murder and had seen the coverage on the news, but I had no idea it was my biological mother! I remember driving myself home that afternoon, slamming my hands against the steering wheel, and wanting to end my life. Thoughts of just driving my car off the road and into a tree were overwhelming. I shouted as loud as

I could, "How could you allow this to happen?! If you really do exist, you are the meanest and worst God ever!"

I had to blame someone. I felt so incredibly empty, lost, hopeless, furious—and I remember my life slowly began to spiral even more out of control from that moment on. The one person I thought would make life worth living, was gone. My one chance of finding true love and finally feeling that mother-daughter connection was now gone, stolen from me. And not because of a random illness or car accident, but because she was murdered. I could not wrap my head around this disturbing thought. What were the chances?

I turned into a bitter, resentful person. I was angry. Beyond angry. The one moment I had dreamt about since I was a little girl was over in a matter of minutes. After many years of waiting for this moment, I had literally just missed her by a couple of months. All because of some selfish jerk, who still to this day is rotting in jail for his reprehensible actions after receiving the maximum sentence—life without parole

I tried to somehow come to a place of acceptance and kept telling myself the one mantra I learned as a kid: 'Things happen for a reason'. And, 'Whatever doesn't kill you makes you stronger'. But did I honestly believe these things? It was beyond difficult to accept. Then I was haunted by all the 'what-if's'. What if she never dated that awful man in the first place? What if I had gone to find her just a few years or even one year earlier? But again, I was left feeling empty. None of these thoughts were going to bring her back and I was forced to accept the simple fact that it just wasn't meant to be.

Life continued to kick me while I was down as I dealt with the dissolution of my first marriage. And in December 2000, I decided to leave everything behind and start anew. So I loaded a few belongings and my dog into my truck, my two horses in a trailer, and down to Florida I drove, in hopes of starting a new life. It was a rocky start and a bit of an adjustment, but over time, my life started to settle. The one thing that would give me the slightest peace, was speaking to both of my deceased mother's. I guess you could call this a form of prayer and I think most would agree that praying/speaking to our deceased loved one's gives many of us peace. Just the thought of them still somehow being with us, provides some comfort. I would often speak silently to them and ask them for help and guidance with certain situations. I held onto some hope that they were looking down on me from heaven and hoping they could see me and help me. I'd also ask them for signs, which sometimes I'd see and sometimes not.

This was a fine coping mechanism, but I still came up short. The simple fact remained—I was emotionally unsettled, distraught and empty. For years I wallowed in self-pity as I focused on how unfair life was. I was continually haunted by the fact that I had no control over the horrific circumstances surrounding my mother's murder, or the timing involved, or the fact that I was given up for adoption in the first place.

But little did I know, God had a plan all along—a master plan that took many years to unravel and still continues to unravel today. A plan that now, believe it or not, I wouldn't change for anything.

Chapter 8

UNAWARE OF HIS PRESENCE

It is safe to say, my relationship with God began in a very hostile manner. As I've mentioned, I knew enough about God to blame Him for everything bad that happened in my life. By the time I hit my early thirties, life had served me with enough heartache and tragedy that I was shaped, molded and hardened into a resentful and bitter person.

But I can't say things were all bad. In 2003, I purchased a small horse farm in Wellington, FL. I was out at my barn one day, gathering up a pile of dirty saddle pads that needed to be washed, when I was hit with a unique design idea. Without hesitation, I went out and bought an old industrial sewing machine, taught myself how to sew and that's when Equine Couture was born. I started manufacturing my own preppy ribbon designs that I'd sew around the border of saddle pads, belts, polo wraps, show shirts and even dog collars. I was the first to bring vibrant color, fun, flair, and fashion to an otherwise mundane and conservative equestrian world. I set up a booth at my first tradeshow in 2004 when some of the largest retail stores and catalog companies in the industry started immediately placing orders for my products. One was even featured on the cover of the SmartPak Equine catalog. Equine Couture became an overnight success.

When I returned home from the tradeshow, I met up with some friends and we all decided, for the fun of it, to visit a well-known psychic in the area whom I had been to before when I was looking for answers and direction in my life. During this particular reading, she told me I had a horse that was going to give birth to a foal, and that foal was going to become a world class jumper. She then said that someone I knew had a perfect stallion to breed her with. Ironically, I did know a local woman who owned a very famous stallion and within a few months, my horse was artificially inseminated. I could not believe how spot-on and specific this psychic lady was and I was filled with such hope and excitement. Horses were my life and they were the one thing that provided me unconditional joy and happiness.

It was April 2005 and my horse was nearing the end of her pregnancy and was due to give birth in just a few weeks. I had married my second husband one year prior and I too had just found out I was five weeks pregnant and we were expecting our first child—life could not have been better!

With just one week remaining in my horse's pregnancy, the unthinkable happened to me—a miscarriage. A couple of my girlfriends had also had miscarriages in the past, so I knew it was fairly common. But it's a completely different ballgame when it actually happens to you. I was truly heartbroken. The loss was almost unbearable. I felt like a complete failure and the thoughts of never being a mother haunted me. Down I went again, another one-two punch.

However, the fast approaching birth of my horse's foal gave me at least a little something to look forward to. Until the night she went into labor. It was 9:00 pm and I could tell she was struggling, so I called my veterinarian. He came and checked her and said everything was fine. He could feel the foal's hooves positioned in the birth canal and he told me to go back inside and just be patient. I did what he said—yet several more hours passed, and my horse was still unable to give birth.

I called him to come out again and by this time it was 3:00 am. As he reached inside the birth canal again, he was shocked to find out that he was feeling the foals back hooves, not the front hooves. The foal was in the breech position and it would not be able to come out on its own. My vet quickly ran to his truck to grab some chains. He proceeded to put the chains inside my horse, wrap them around the back legs of the foal and then proceeded to pull as hard as he could.

As he fought long and hard against my horse's uterine muscles, which had tightly closed around the foal, he finally gave one last pull as the foal's lifeless body fell to the ground with a thug.

Once again, the unthinkable happened—the foal was born dead. By the time my vet was finally able to get it out, it had suffocated within my horse. It was too late. That was it. I was done. Physically and emotionally distraught and exhausted. I could barely gasp for air beneath my tears. I fell to the ground and with the last bit of energy I could muster, I began to scream and shout out to the black sky in hopes that someone would hear me.

I first cursed out that psychic woman for giving me false hope and saying I should breed my horse in the first place, as I vowed to never go to her again. I then shouted at God—again I told Him how much I hated Him. And if He really did exist, how sick and evil I thought He was. It was disgusting. My life was filled with some decent highs which were always followed by the lowest of lows. What kind of sick, twisted life was this? What was this stupid life all about? Why was I even born and why was I even here?

Another year went by and it was January 2006. I flew with a friend of mine to Atlantic City for another wholesale tradeshow to sell my Equine Couture products. This was my third equestrian tradeshow and I was looking forward to another successful show. I was also six months along in another pregnancy. Luckily, I was past the miscarriage stage and far enough along to have hope that nothing would go wrong with this pregnancy.

We arrived at the convention center and went right to work setting up the booth. The next day, the tradeshow began, and halfway through the day, I left the booth to go grab us some lunch. As I walked up and down the aisles, something was odd. I was noticing familiar designs being sold by many of the larger companies (my competition) that looked almost exactly like mine. They were all selling knockoffs of my designs—at half the price. Panic immediately set in and I felt nauseous. I was standing face-to-face with my worst fear. I had spoken to several attorney's when I first started my business, to see if there was any way I could patent, copyright or protect my designs. But unfortunately, there was no way to protect my designs; and is the reason why we see so many high-end designer brand knockoffs.

I had a good run with my designs for the past two years and now the other companies had caught on. In my gut, I knew my time was up.

As I welled up with tears, I made a beeline to the nearest restroom and fell to the floor. Once again, I was utterly crushed and defeated. I surely could not handle another blow like this. I began pounding the cement with my fists as tears poured from my eyes. I screamed, "God! I have had enough! I cannot take it anymore! If you truly exist, you have to do something! You know how long and how hard I've been working for this, and are you really going to let the big guy squash the little guy? Seriously? You have to do something!"

I had just finished my temper-tantrum, when a woman walked into the bathroom and saw that I was clearly upset. She asked if I was okay, noticed I was pregnant, and then asked if I was going into labor, and if she should call for emergency help. Feeling embarrassed, I quietly responded, "No, I'm fine." I then picked myself up off the floor, wiped away my tears with a paper towel, and walked back to my booth. As soon as I returned, my friend took one look at me and could instantly tell that something was wrong. She asked if I was okay.

"No, I'm not okay!" and I proceeded to tell her how I had seen several companies selling knockoffs of my designs for half the price. She said she too had noticed but was afraid to say anything to me.

A few minutes later I was talking to another woman, explaining my situation to her, and she immediately grabbed my hand and led me to a booth where she introduced me to an employee at JPC Equestrian, the largest manufacturer and distributor in the industry. After we spoke for a bit, I returned to my booth, and not even ten minutes later, the owner of JPC Equestrian, Varun (Timmy) Sharma, approached me and asked if we could speak. He said that he had seen the success of my business and that my designs would add the fashion that his company was lacking. He then asked if I would consider joining forces with him, adding, "And your designs are nothing without you, so not only would I like to buy your company, but would you also consider traveling to India twice each year to work on new designs with my factories?"

I was shocked. And as I stared at him with a puzzled look on my face, I began to slowly look around the convention hall because I felt like I was being pranked! I then asked him, "Are you serious, is this a joke?" He smiled and calmly said "No, this is not a joke." He then looked into my eyes and earnestly continued, "If we can have a business relationship based on trust and respect for one another, I think we will be hugely successful." His words pierced my soul. A relationship based on trust and respect? No man had ever said those words to me before. I immediately felt a sense of peace and thought to myself, "Could God have answered my desperate prayer in just a matter of minutes? Seriously?"

Considering I was a science major in college, the mere thought of an answered prayer made zero logical sense to me. I am a, 'show me', kind of gal. I won't believe anything or anyone until I have tangible proof by seeing with my own eyes. Although this appeared to be that tangible proof, I quickly labeled it a coincidence and soon forgot about my '10-minute answer to prayer' moment and never gave it another thought. Within one month, I signed all the paperwork for the sale of my company and my new role as designer was underway.

The timing of this merger was perfect because three months later, my daughter was born. This was a beautiful moment for me as it satisfied that biological mother-daughter bond I had missed out on as a child. Yet it wasn't long after she was born that my life started to quickly unravel once again.

I could sense something wasn't quite right with my second husband, who I will refer to as Steve. I knew something in our relationship had changed. He was distant, cold, strange, and different. Time and time again I would ask him if everything was ok and he would always assure me it was. He had a bit of a drinking problem and I tried to give him an out by suggesting that maybe he drank too much one night and something happened—and if so, I would understand as long as he could just come clean. But he continually denied everything and kept insisting that nothing was going on. The more I asked, the angrier and more defensive he became. It got to the point where he was calling me crazy for asking such things and I was beginning to believe him.

Then, the day came when I found some inappropriate emails he had written to other women as well as some provocative websites he had been looking at. I confronted him about this. Even though the evidence was right there in front of him, he still tried to deny it. It was absurd.

Our baby girl was just a couple months old and every night after she fell asleep, I would go out to the barn for night-check. I'd clean out my horse's stalls and give them each one last flake of hay for the night. The barn was my sanctuary, my happy place. One night, Steve and I had another heated argument and this one was bad. So while I was out at the barn cleaning stalls, I decided to pray once again—like I did in the Atlantic City Convention Center bathroom. However, this prayer was much simpler, and less dramatic. I just said it in my head: "God, I know something is going on with Steve, I just know it. Can you please make him tell me what is going on? I need to hear the truth and I am ready to hear it."

I finished my nightly chores, gave my horses one last kiss on their noses, shut the lights off to the barn, and walked back to the house. I crawled into bed with Steve who was already asleep and as soon as my head hit the pillow, I too was out. A few hours later, he woke up in a panic. "Laurie," he said, "call 911 quick! Something is wrong with me! I think I'm having a heart attack!" I quickly sat up and fumbled for my phone. I turned toward him and asked, "What's going on? Are you in pain?" He shouted, "No, I just can't breathe!"

I slowly put my phone back down on the nightstand and looked at him as he sat breathing heavily on the side of the bed. I confidently yet calmly said, "I don't think you're having a heart attack, I think you're having an anxiety attack." He sat with his head down, breathing heavily. I asked, "Am I right Steve?" There was no reply. He continued to sit on the side of the bed without saying a word. At that moment, I knew what was going on—I knew I was finally going to get my answers. After about 20 minutes of us both sitting there silent and motionless, I calmly asked, "So, is there something you want to tell me?" He continued to sit in silence, in the dark, for what seemed like an hour. I patiently waited and asked him again, "Is there something you want to tell me?" In a cracked voice, he finally replied, "Yes." I sat there and waited and waited and waited, until he quietly said, "Remember that business trip I took to Connecticut?"

"Yeah."

"Well, I just want you to know I got really drunk one night and slept with a prostitute."

And so, the purging began. He then continued to tell me more stories of other times spent with prostitutes—as well as a situation where he was alone with our daughter, who, at the time, was less than a year old. It was then I realized that once again, my prayer at the barn that night was answered in just a matter of hours. Again, there appeared to be tangible proof of an answered prayer. Steve awoke out of a sound sleep that night, as if literally shaken by the fear of God, and forced to tell me the truth.

More and more stories came pouring out of his mouth like a flowing river. It seemed the more he told me, the lighter his load became and the better he felt. Unfortunately, the more he shared with me, the heavier my emotional load became and although my prayer was answered, hearing the truth was overwhelming as my heart began to race uncontrollably and I felt nauseous.

Then, as I sat there trying my best to remain mentally calm, I was hit with another wave of emotion, but this time I was overcome with a supernatural feeling of peace—as if an invisible barrier surrounded and protected me emotionally. My heart rate slowed, and the nausea went away. I never got mad, angry, sad or upset. I sat there quietly, void of emotion, just listening to every little detail he continued spewing. Stuff he did back when he was a teenager. He told me everything. I sat calmly and quietly with such peace and clarity as one simple thought raced through my mind, "I am so out of here. I am ending this marriage immediately and taking my daughter with me!"

The fear of being a single parent was now my reality. How would I do it on my own? I had no family or close friends living nearby. I was alone. But I didn't have a choice and somehow, someway, I was going to have to do it. And strangely enough, I had peace with it. I somehow knew my daughter and I were going to be okay.

The next day, the sadness and pain of Steve's betrayal had really set in. I needed someone to talk to, so I confided in a neighbor whom I barely knew. She was a very sweet, older, motherly-type woman who was kind enough to listen and quite empathetic toward my situation. However, sharing the details with her never made me feel any better and certainly didn't make my sadness and pain go away.

The following Saturday afternoon there was a knock at my front door. It was my sweet neighbor whom I had just confided in. She asked if she could come in. We sat down and she said, "I've been thinking so much about everything you told me and I'm kind of blown away. Do you realize God has not once, but twice, vividly answered your prayers?" I glared at her with a confused look. Here I was thinking she was there to see how I was doing, and instead, she blindsides me with this.

Again, she asked, "Laurie do you realize this?" She continued, "The time in Atlantic City when you prayed in the bathroom and then almost immediately met the man from India who bought your company, and now with this. I have been a Christian for many years, and I can't say that God has this vividly shown up in my life, if ever!"

"Yeah, I guess it's a little coincidental," I said.

She corrected me saying, "Well, surely you cannot call this a coincidence. You shared with me two dramatic stories where you took a moment to pray specifically about two different situations and God vividly showed up both times. Please tell me you are not going to dismiss this as a coincidence."

Almost wanting to appease her, I reluctantly agreed and said, "Yeah, I guess you're right".

I must admit, what she said to me that day did make me take a step back and think for a moment, but the reality of God never quite hit me. I brushed it aside, quickly changed the subject and offered her a drink as I walked toward the kitchen. She followed me and sat at my counter. As I handed her a drink, she asked, "Would you like to come to church with me tonight?" I immediately laughed out loud and boldly said, "No, I do not. It'll be a cold day in hell before I step foot in a church again!" She looked at me wide-eyed, clearly not expecting that response. But she calmly leaned forward in her chair and said, "Laurie, I may not know you well, but I think I know you well enough to know you will like my church."

For some reason, the way she looked at me and the way in which she spoke was convincing enough that I decided to go. At that point, I figured I had nothing else to lose. So, I got myself and my daughter dressed, and we drove together that evening to Christ Fellowship.

As we turned into this massive parking lot, a huge, non-churchy looking building stood before us. I remember thinking I had never seen a church like this before. We walked in and everyone was so over-the-top friendly and welcoming—a foreign feeling and experience for me.

We were ushered toward a massive auditorium where I could hear loud music playing. As the doors opened, the music hit me like a tidal wave. Not only was it loud, but it was vibrant, amazing, and moving. It was a live band performing with live singers. It was as if I was walking into a rock concert but, somehow, better.

The wave of music hit me emotionally as I felt my eyes uncontrollably well-up with tears. I felt embarrassed and a bit uncomfortable as I tried hard to hold back the tears. But this music was too powerful. My sweet little neighbor grabbed my hand, looked me in the eye and gave me a warm smile. I had no idea what was happening and why I was crying. Even though my mind didn't recognize the music or the lyrics, my soul somehow did, triggering a flood of happy tears.

After the music ended and the band members left the stage, the pastor appeared, wearing tan pants and a blue polo shirt. I thought to myself, "This is odd, where's the priest in his robe?"

The pastor then spoke of his wife and children. Wife and children? Again, I was shocked. I knew priests took a vow of celibacy and were not allowed to be married so this again was a foreign concept to me. He was an older, super-cool guy who was an ex-football coach. And that's how he spoke, like a coach! Being an avid soccer player my entire life and throughout college, this was something I could surely relate to. I couldn't tell you what he spoke about; all I knew is I loved it. And it was as if he was speaking directly to me. It was basically a motivational speech based on Biblical principles. His words were the medicine I needed to hear after the overwhelming shock and heartache I had just been through. So much so that I kept going back week after week.

However, one thing that was slightly annoying was how the pastor would continually mention the name of Jesus. Who was this Jesus anyway? Hearing the name would almost make me cringe. The continuous mention of Jesus was a bit much, as was him mentioning we should read the Bible and study God's word. What did that even mean? Why would that be so important? All I knew was reading the Bible would never be an option for me. Yet I continued to go because I would always leave feeling so much better, optimistic and hopeful.

Several weeks later, I was walking my daughter in her stroller through my neighborhood. I was introduced, by a mutual friend, to another neighbor named Sierra. She was a young gal in her mid-twenties who also had a baby girl about the same age as mine. She and I hit it off immediately. One day, Sierra graciously offered to watch my daughter once a week for a couple of hours, so I could run errands and do some grocery shopping. With no family or any help, I jumped at the offer!

By the third week, I had gotten to know Sierra well and I loved how much fun our daughters had playing together. As I was leaving her house one day, she asked me if I'd like to join her at a Bible study on Wednesday mornings. I politely declined.

Another week went by and she asked me a second time. Again, I said, "No thanks Sierra, that's really not for me, I'm truly not interested."

Another week went by and she actually had the nerve to ask me a third time. By this time, I was so taken aback by her audacity that I curtly replied, "Fine Sierra, just to shut you up, I'll go!"

So off I went. I remember entering the room that first Wednesday morning and feeling like the odd ball out. Remember the song from Sesame Street: One of these things is not like the others… one of these things just doesn't belong? Well, that pretty much sums up how I was feeling as I walked into the room that morning. It was clear, at least to me, that I did not belong. The room was filled with about 30 women who were nothing like me. They were mostly older women with a few younger ones mixed in and everyone was overly friendly and welcoming. So much so that I thought to myself, "These women are so fake", which made me feel even more awkward. So I stuck close to Sierra and sat with her as she introduced me to the other six women sitting at the table.

A much older woman named Janice was the table leader. She was a very sweet grandma-type woman who seemed quite knowledgeable. I remember they were studying the Book of Psalms. I really didn't understand what they were talking about, but it was fine. I glanced throughout the room to see if there were any other potential friend candidates. I noticed a cute, dark-haired girl who looked like my type of friend. I asked Sierra if she knew her and after the Bible Study was over, she introduced me to her. Her name was Lena. I spoke with her for a bit and she told me she also had a daughter just one year older than mine, and a son three years older. Even though I felt out of place, I continued going back to that Bible Study week after week and my friendships with Sierra and Lena strengthened.

One morning in particular, I walked into Bible study, sat at our usual table and that was the day we began discussing how women should submit to their husbands. Needless to say, after everything I just went through with my soon-to-be-ex, this was the last thing I wanted to hear, so I boldly spoke up and said, "I just want to say that this is a subject I completely disagree with."

Janice, the sweet older woman looked at me and gently said, "Now dear, this may not make sense to you now, but someday it will." I quickly snapped back and said, "This will never make sense to me and I will never submit to any man." She just looked at me and smiled. Not a smug smile but a genuine sweet smile. As did the other women in the room. Even though I was all fired up and ready for a verbal battle, no one even tried to cram it down my throat or convince me otherwise. They all just left it alone and moved on, which immediately diffused the verbal bomb that was about to explode from my mouth.

The following week I walked into Bible Study and Janice approached me with a big smile on her face as she handed me a Bible. She said it was a gift she wanted me to have. I reluctantly thanked her as I thought to myself, "Oh great, what am I supposed to do with this thing?"

It had now been two months since Steve's confessions and my next business trip to India was fast approaching. I clearly did not trust Steve and did not want to leave ParisElla alone with him. I thought long and hard about cancelling the trip. I agonized and wrestled with the decision, but this trip was unlike any other and was extremely important. I was working with another company on a project and they were sending a representative named Melanie to India with me to work on it.

The first year after selling my business was fine. But the ten-percent commission I was receiving each month on my designs was nothing compared to the thousands I was making each month on my own. I could no longer afford my house or my horses. My daughter was my priority, so I put everything up for sale. I was able to sell one of my horses rather quickly, but I knew the other one would be much harder to sell—she wasn't the nicest or easiest horse to ride. My house had been on the market for two years and with no legitimate buyers, it was only a matter of time before that would go into foreclosure. I had pretty much hit rock-bottom. I picked up a part-time waitressing job just to earn enough money to feed my daughter and make ends meet each week.

I had a phone conversation with my boss Timmy, prior to my trip, asking him, since I was now going to be a single mom, if I could please receive a little more than just the ten percent commission. After having been to India a few times and seeing the opulence that surrounded Timmy, I was sure he would agree. But instead, he gave me a cold, hard 'no' and said, "That's not what we agreed upon in the contract." I continued stating my case and stressing to him the severity of my situation and how my life took an unexpected turn for the worst. Only to realize that everything I was saying was falling on deaf ears. I quickly became frustrated and angry and after fifteen minutes of arguing with him, I realized that nothing I said was going to change his mind. I hung up and immediately regretted selling my business to him and that is when my anger and hatred toward him ignited.

So here I was, presented with a golden opportunity to work with this other company on a new project that could potentially provide me with extra income. Something at the time I could not refuse, so cancelling the trip was not an option. I just needed to find a trustworthy and safe place for ParisElla to stay while I was away. I remember standing in my front yard, once again crying profusely, looking up to that big black sky and realizing yet again, the lack of control I had over anything.

Then the thought of my new-found friend Lena popped into my head. Even though we had only known each other a short time, I felt an instant connection and special bond with her. She and her husband were people I could surely trust. I vividly remember calling her that night and asking if she would mind watching ParisElla for me for the ten days I would be away. She felt awkward saying yes and expressed obvious concerns about Steve. But after discussing with her husband, they agreed, knowing how important it was to me.

The night before I was to leave, I told Steve that ParisElla was going to be staying with someone else while I was away. He immediately flipped out as our conversation quickly escalated into a huge argument. He insisted on watching her while I was away, and I made it very clear he was not going to. It got to the point where I secretly packed-up all her necessities and literally snuck her out the back door. I then quickly jumped into my car and drove to Lena's house thinking, "How could my life have come to this?"

I dropped Paris off with Lena and her family. I thanked her profusely for doing this for me. She was quite compassionate and understanding but out of slight concern, she did ask me once again if I was sure Steve didn't know where they lived. I not only assured her of that but also that he didn't even know their names. She then changed the subject and asked how long my flight was to India and I told her almost twenty-four hours. She was a bit shocked and said, "Well I hope you brought enough books to read on the flight."

"Well sort of, I am bringing one book with me," I said. Lena asked which one. I said, "The Bible." She laughed and said, "Alrighty then, good luck with that!" By that point, she knew me well enough to know I was far from God, so the mere thought of me bringing a Bible was laughable. However, being as competitive as I am, I took her response as a personal challenge and immediately thought to myself, "Game on! How difficult could it be anyway?"

I gave ParisElla one last kiss goodbye and off I went.

Chapter 9
TEXT MESSAGE FROM GOD

I arrived at the airport with perfect peace knowing ParisElla was in good hands with Lena and her family. I met Melanie, the woman I was working on the project with, in the Newark airport and we boarded the flight together to India. When we arrived in New Delhi, we were picked up by a driver who dropped us off at my boss, Timmy's farmhouse, where we would stay for the duration of our trip.

Day in and day out, Melanie and I worked closely with the design team at the factory on the development of our new project. I went into this trip, still holding onto some resentment toward Timmy for refusing to increase my monthly commission. So, during one of our meetings, Timmy and I once again exchanged some not-so-pleasant words. I was so upset, I ended up leaving the conference room and was later told that he announced to everyone that I must be a nightmare to be married to. How sweet. What a wonderful thing to hear. It took everything in me not to lose my cool, but my feelings were clear, I legitimately despised this man. Now, with everything I had just been through back home coupled with this hatred toward my boss, that oh-so-familiar feeling of despair engulfed me once again, as I felt like the entire world was against me. Could I just catch a break for crying out loud?

The more time I spent with Melanie, the more I would confide in her. I told her how nervous I was, coming on this trip to India, leaving my daughter behind and the situation that had just transpired with her father. She and I became quite close as she too shared some of her own personal affairs.

At the time, I owned a modest flip phone that had no international roaming or service. Needless to say, I was not able to receive calls, make calls, or send or receive text messages. Melanie on the other hand, had one of those fancy (at the time) Blackberry phones. She of course had international roaming and was kind enough to let me use her phone each day so I could call Lena and check on Paris-Ella. This gave me great peace of mind.

After work, Melanie and I would grab a quick bite to eat for dinner and then we were driven back to the farmhouse where we would part ways. I to my bedroom and she to hers.

Every night before bed, I would pick up my Bible, which I kept on the nightstand, and attempt to read it. 'Attempt' being the key word. I soon realized why Lena found such humor in me saying I was going to start reading the Bible. I tried starting at the beginning, the Book of Genesis. At first it made sense, sort of, but as I continued reading, it became more and more confusing. So I flipped to the New Testament toward the back, where I might as well have been reading Greek. Night after night, I tried reading but continued to fall short. I was not even remotely understanding what I was reading and couldn't help but wonder what all this hype was with the Bible anyway. My competitive bubble quickly burst as I happily threw in the towel. I smiled as I thought of Lena saying to me, "Good luck with that!" She was right.

Our time in India flew by and we had just one day left. It was Friday, March 21, 2008. Melanie and I had accomplished what we set out to do on this trip and we both were excited for the launch of this new product.

That day, I tried calling Lena for my daily check-in and for some reason she didn't answer. I didn't think too much about it until I tried calling again just before we ate dinner and still no answer. I started to get a little nervous, wondering if everything was okay. We were dropped off at the farmhouse after dinner and my mind was a bit frazzled and concerned. Before parting ways to our separate rooms, Melanie told me not to worry and reminded me that we would be heading home the next night. She was right. So I got into bed, slid under the sheets and shut the light off. Within minutes I drifted to sleep. That is, until my cell phone started ringing.

It was 2:32 a.m., the day we were leaving to go back home, when oddly enough, my cell phone on the nightstand next to my bed began to ring and ring and ring, waking me out of a sound sleep. I had no idea how it was ringing since I had no roaming or international service the entire time in India. Still half asleep, and very confused, I leaned over, grabbed my phone and hazily said, "Hello?" A woman's voice on the other end said, "Hi, is so and so there?" (I can't remember the name she asked for.) "No, you must have the wrong number," I said and hung up.

Still confused, I closed my flip phone and put it back on the nightstand. As soon as I laid my head on the pillow, my phone lit up the room. I picked it up again and saw that I had a text message. I thought to myself, "This cannot be possible". I had no service and was not able to send or receive text messages. I opened the message. It read: '1 jn 5 12 hopin and prayin'. I read and dismissed it, assuming it was from the same woman who had just called. Plus, it was filled with a bunch of typos that didn't make any sense.

I set the phone back down on the nightstand and tried to fall back asleep. However, by this point, I was wide awake. So much so that as soon as I tried to close my eyes, they would pop right back open. Instead, I laid there wide-awake, as a crazy thought popped into my head. I shot up, turned the bedside lamp on, and read that text again. Could this have been a scripture that someone texted to me? My Bible was on the same nightstand next to my phone. I didn't know much about the Bible, but I did know that 'jn' was an abbreviation for John. So I flipped through the pages until I found the *Book of John*. I began reading the first chapter, since the text said '1 jn 5 12' and read all the verses including verses 5 through 12. It was a short chapter so I read it over and over again hoping it would eventually make some sense to me, but to no avail, I gave up.

I closed the Bible, put it back on the nightstand, shut off the light, and tried once again to fall asleep. My mind was racing. The thought of not getting through to Lena that day began haunting me. Was my daughter okay? Did something happen to her? Crazy, scary thoughts then plagued me. What if Steve found out where she was? Panic set in. My mind went to a dark place as I convinced myself that Steve had somehow found Lena's house, took ParisElla, killed her, and then killed himself. I was sure that was why she didn't answer her phone.

I turned on the light and tried calling Lena. Since it just rang and I just received a text message, surely it would work now if I tried calling her. But soon after I dialed her number I heard that voice saying, "Your number cannot be completed as dialed." Seriously? And with it now being almost 3 a.m., I couldn't possibly go across the hall to Melanie's room and ask to borrow her phone. The one time I just needed to hear Lena's voice telling me all was okay. But no. Panic, hopelessness and fear overwhelmed me. There was nothing I could do. It was another situation where I had zero control. I shut the light off and laid back down. As I stared up at the ceiling, I was gripped with fear and could literally hear and feel my heart pounding out of my chest. The feeling was awful, and I was on the verge of a panic attack.

Then, out of nowhere, I heard a voice within my head say: "It's Okay, just tell them to leave."

"What the heck? Tell who to leave?" I thought.

The voice continued, "Tell them to go away, tell them they are not wanted here." Was I going mad? I couldn't for the life of me, figure out what was going on but out of sheer desperation, I did what I was told and started repeating over and over in a soft voice, "Go away; go away; go away, go away. You're not wanted here. Go away; go away, go away."

The more I said it, the better I surprisingly started to feel. I lay there in shock. Then, I was hit with the most profound realization; and as crazy as this may sound, I thought to myself, "God, is that you?"

Immediately I heard the voice say, "Yes my child." Right then and there, in my mind's eye, the brightest light appeared right above me. I sobbed. Tears flowed like a river. Overwhelming and intensely happy tears. "But why?" I asked. "Why are you talking to me? And why of all places are you talking to me here in India?"

"It's because of Melanie. There is something I want you to tell her."

"Okay, what do you want me to tell her?"

"Tell her that I love her, tell her that God loves her." I paused and reluctantly replied, "Okay?"

A bigger question then popped into my mind but before I could form the words, I heard the voice say, "Yes, your daughter is just fine."

The relief was overwhelming as tears of pure joy poured from my eyes. A few minutes passed and the strangest thing happened: I laid there staring up at the ceiling as if I was watching a movie reel with a series of short clips. I was shown every bad situation I ever went through, starting with my early childhood. And with each clip I saw, He would then remove it and take it away. It was as if He were erasing those bad memories and experiences from my past. Cleaning my slate. The more he showed me, the more He took away, and the better I began to feel. With every negative emotion those situations invoked, he continuously removed them and replaced and filled each with His love. The feeling was surreal and the only way I can describe it is a feeling of complete and perfect love.

It was in that moment that I realized He had been with me all along. He had been by my side throughout it all. He was with me during the worst of the worst times. For the first time in my life, I felt complete. It was He who I had been looking for all along. He was the love I had been missing and was searching for my entire life. And I was so in awe, so humbled, so overwhelmed by this feeling of complete love. It was euphoric. I felt so joyful and light, like I was levitating off the bed.

At this point I asked, "What can I do now? What can I do for you? Should I go work at a church? At Christ Fellowship? What do you want me to do?"

"You have a special way about you, and I will bring them to you. People will come to you," He said. "And if you do everything I ask of you, you will be rewarded greatly," He added.

I thought, "This sure sounds strange and doesn't make much sense, but okay…"

The conversation continued for a couple of hours and before I knew it, it was 6:30 a.m. The sun was starting to rise. I sat up and turned on the lamp on the nightstand. I picked up my Bible and again read the first chapter of the Book of John. As if before I was blind, I was now able to see because I understood what I was reading. John 1:5-12, reads as follows:

"The light shines in the darkness, and the darkness can never extinguish it. God sent a man, John the Baptist, to tell about the light so that everyone might believe because of his testimony. John himself was not the light; he was simply a witness to tell about the light. The one who is the true light, who gives light to everyone, was coming into the world. He came into the very world he created, but the world didn't recognize him. He came to his own people, and even they rejected him. But to all who believed him and accepted him, he gave the right to become children of God. They are re-born, born-again—not with a physical birth resulting from human passion or plan, but a birth that comes from God."

Wow. Could it be? Was this Biblical validation for exactly what I had just experienced? I literally had a full-blown conversation with Jesus Himself. I subconsciously recognized His voice. As it is written in John 10:14, Jesus said, "I am the good shepherd; I know my sheep and my sheep know me... they recognize my voice."

But the one thing that stood out was the born-again part. Did it really say I was born-again? Me? No! It cannot be! I did not want to be one of those! One of those born-again freaks! As soon as I realized this passage could very well be referring to me, I closed my Bible and slammed it down on the nightstand.

I stood up and began pacing the room. I nervously thought, "I do not want to be one of those born-again freaks. No. No. No. I said to myself, "And there is no way on earth I am going to tell Melanie that God loves her. No way!" I paced the room more and more frantically as I began to nervously crack my knuckles. Melanie and I were in the same line of work and we had many mutual colleagues. If I tell her this, she's going to think I'm a crazy lunatic and then she's going to tell everyone else we know that I'm crazy. No way was I going to tell her that!

As if an invisible force pushed me out of my room, I found myself knocking on Melanie's door at 6:40 in the morning. Melanie answered the door, barely able to open her eyes. "What is it Laurie? Are you ok?" She asked.

"No Melanie, I'm not ok, I said."

"Come on in, what's going on?" I sat on the edge of her bed and before I had time to talk myself out of it, the words started flowing from my mouth.

"Melanie, I have to tell you something. But what I'm about to tell you is beyond all comprehension. You have to promise me you are going to have an open mind with what I'm about to say right now."

Before I could even finish my sentence, Melanie gasped for air, rose to her feet, covered her hands to her mouth, and started shaking her head as she stared at me with disbelief.

"Melanie what's wrong?" I asked.

"I know what you're going to tell me, I know what you're going to say," she said.

I started to smile as I smugly assured her otherwise. "Melanie, there is no possible way you could know what I'm about to tell you."

Melanie fell to her knees and started to cry. "But I do, I do know what you're going to say," she said.

I started to get a little annoyed and sarcastically responded, "Okay Melanie, if you know what I'm going to say then tell me."

She burst out in tears and exclaimed, "God has a message for me, doesn't He? He wants you to tell me that He loves me!"

My eyes widened and my entire body started shaking as I stared at her in complete disbelief. I felt like I was about to throw up. My knee-jerk reaction was anger. I looked around the room and shouted, "Are you freaking kidding me Melanie? Is this some sick joke? Seriously? I am so freaked out right now!" Once again, I felt like I was being pranked.

As she continued to cry, I asked her, "How the heck did you know what I was going to tell you? Especially something as far-fetched as a message from God?"

Melanie then explained that this was not the first time this had happened to her. I was actually the third person sent into her life with this same message. She slowly got up off the floor and sat on the edge of her bed. I sat down beside her in complete silence and utter shock.

After several minutes passed, I quietly said, "Melanie, do you have any idea what is going on? This trip to India we took together had nothing to do with this silly little project we were working on. There is a far greater thing going on out there. Do you see it?"

"Yes, I know," she replied. Again, we sat in silence and in complete awe of what had just happened. We were both drained emotionally but knew with the sun now almost fully up, we had a full day of work ahead of us before our flight home that evening.

Life as I knew it had changed. I was overwhelmed with so many different emotions and for the first time I felt so small. My existence felt so meaningless and trivial compared to the magnificence I now knew existed out there beyond our mind's comprehension. The reality of a God that truly does exist, combined with the complete control He had with the series of events leading up to this India trip, highlighting what little control I had.

The complete power He had as I received a phone call to wake me up, followed by a text message I was meant to read. All on a phone that had no service the entire time I was in India. And His complete majesty, as I was graced by the presence of our Mighty God. The Creator of the entire universe actually cares and loves me so much that He allowed me to experience something that He knew I needed—that tangible proof, once and for all, of how real He is. What pristine choreography. I knew right then and there that my life would be different. That I would be different. To experience what I just had was a true gift. One which I was ready to embrace and one that I had been unknowingly waiting for and searching for, my entire life.

That day, Melanie and I could barely say two words to each other. We both remained in a state of shock. It was our final day at the factory and our flight home was scheduled to leave New Delhi that night. I, more than ever, was so excited to get home to my baby girl. While driving to the factory I had so many questions running through my mind. As I pondered the happenings from just a few hours prior, I asked Melanie if we could use her phone to call the number that had sent me the text message. Me being the curious cat that I am, I wanted to test once again the reality of what had transpired. So I showed her the text message and she dialed the number associated with it. It rang twice and then went to a voice saying: "The number you have reached is not accepting calls at this time. Please try again later."

I had never heard that message before. I had only heard the messages that say the number was no longer in service or has been disconnected. But I had never heard that the number you have reached is not accepting calls at this time. She and I tried calling the number several times throughout the day and even continued trying several days and weeks later and never did get through to anyone which to me, was even more validation.

Our flight home went smoothly, and I drove directly to Lena's house after arriving at the PBI Airport. When Lena opened the door, I could not hold back my tears. I gave her the biggest hug, thanked her so much for watching ParisElla, and then quickly darted around the corner to find my baby girl, who was almost two years old at the time. I called out her name and knelt down with open arms as she came running toward me from the playroom. She had a huge smile on her face.

"Mama, mama," she exclaimed. She ran into my arms and I squeezed her so tight. I didn't want to let go but she pushed back to get a good look at my face. She stared at me with her big green eyes, noticed I was crying, and started wiping my tears with her tiny little fingers. With the softest little voice, she said, "It okay Mommy, it okay." It was as if she were fully aware of the emotional rollercoaster I had just stepped off from. Then she hugged me once again before she toddled off to play with Lena's daughter.

I stood up and looked at Lena. She asked me if I was ok. "Man, oh man, have I got a story for you guys," I said. Lena and her husband sat down at the table with me.

At this point, I assumed these crazy God experiences were the norm for all Christians. So I didn't hesitate to share every detail with them. I began with how my phone, which had no service, began ringing at 2:32 in the morning, followed by the text message. I could tell Lena's husband was starting to feel a little uneasy. When I began divulging the meaty part of the story, of how Jesus spoke to me, that was when he politely excused himself from the table. Lena continued to hear me out. As I got to the end of my story and how Melanie and I tried calling the number but couldn't get through to anyone, I then asked, "This type of thing happens to all Christians right?"

Lena burst out with the loudest laugh and said, "No honey, not at all! As a matter of fact, I have never heard such a crazy story!"

"Are you serious?" I exclaimed.

"Yeah, I'm dead serious," she said. "This has to be one of the craziest things I've ever heard."

I was completely taken aback and somewhat confused by her response; yet all I could say was, "Well, I guess it's official. I am a legit Born-Again Christian!" I explained to her that I even went back and re-read the scripture from the text message and it actually made sense to me. How I was a new believer in Christ and how I was re-born. Lena asked, "Can I see the text message?"

"Sure," I replied as I pulled out my phone and showed it to her. She looked at it as if she was studying it. Then she said, "I am so sorry to tell you this, but this text says '1 jn 5 12.'"

"Yeah I know."

"Well you told me you went to your Bible and read a passage from the *Book of John*, but this text message is regarding scripture from *1 John*.

"Wait, what? What do you mean?" I asked.

"1 John is an entirely separate book of the Bible, and not the same as the Book of John. So, you basically read the wrong scripture," she said.

The wind in my sails instantly vanished. I immediately began to second guess everything that had happened. I was such a newbie Bible reader that I had no idea there was even a book called, 1 John. And then to later find out there are also the books —2 John and 3 John. Who would know that?

Lena rose from her chair and said, "Hold on, let me go get my Bible." She slowly walked back to the kitchen and as she was reading, she stopped in the doorway.

"Huh," she said.

"What?" I asked.

"This is so strange," she replied. Lena began to read aloud the scripture 1 John 5:12: "Whoever has the son has life, whoever does not have the son does not have life."

She then looked at me and said, "I cannot believe that this scripture is a perfect summation of exactly what did happen to you that night. So everything you read in the Book of John, Chapter 1 is summed up perfectly in this one sentence."

A huge smile came across my face as I exclaimed, "Well wouldn't you know! God already knew I was completely clueless when it came to the Bible so He had to text me scripture that no matter how I looked it up, it would still have the same meaning. Go figure!"

"Yup, pretty much!" Lena said.

We laughed together. "That's pretty crazy when you think about it right? Of all the hundreds of thousands of different scriptures throughout the Bible, what are the chances that these two would say the exact same thing?" I asked.

"Well that's God for ya!" Lena replied.

Days turned into weeks and even months later I was still on, what I call, my 'God-high'. However, as time went on, the battle within my mind began. Thoughts came into my head, trying to convince me that none of it ever happened and that it was all just a dream. But one fact remained; I was always able to fall back on Melanie. For her to know what I was going to say before I even said it—especially when it was about God. She has always been and always will be the validation I needed to remind myself of the reality of what happened that night in India when I received a text message from God.

Chapter 10

THE CURE

All of us, no matter who we are, where we were born or where we live, are searching for something. Something to fulfill us. To fill that missing piece, or void, within each of us. We might search for this 'something' in our jobs, our spouses, our children, our partners, our friends or even in ourselves and inevitably we will come up short.

So let me ask you: are you sick of life being so darn difficult? Because I know I was! Are you fed up and exhausted from trying to make things easy and pleasant, only to have them turn out hard and messy? Are you searching for something better? Do you sometimes feel stranded in the middle of the ocean—treading water, gasping for air, becoming more and more tired as the waves of life pummel you?

Are you mourning the loss of a loved one? Are you being discriminated against? Or suffering with a family issue, a health issue, financial matters, faith matters, or has someone hurt you and let you down? Maybe you struggle with an alcohol addiction, drug addiction, or sex addiction. Maybe someone abused you; either mentally, physically or sexually.

Are you holding onto past shame, regret or guilt? Or you keep trying to climb the ladder of success and are getting nowhere. Maybe you're struggling in a relationship or in your marriage. Are you perhaps a control freak? Maybe your child is dealing with some difficult stuff: being bullied at school, peer pressure or failing to fit in. Perhaps you have periods of depression or thoughts of suicide.

Maybe you live with fear, worry, anxiety or have sleepless nights. And rightly so with this global COVID-19 pandemic that has shaken the entire world to its core.

Whatever it is, you are not alone. Because need I say, life is difficult for all of us. At any given moment, we all will experience at least one or perhaps all of these symptoms of *Spiritual Cancer*. People will hurt us, whether intentionally or unintentionally and we can't force them to apologize, to change, to make up for it, or even admit they did wrong. We can only control how we react. We all will make mistakes and if we make a wrong choice or act foolishly, we must live with the consequences, no matter how bitter they may be.

We may try to live with hidden little secrets, and sometimes our conscience becomes so cold and hardened that our wrong actions don't even bother us. This form of imperfection (sin) thrives in the dark and will continue to eat us alive. We all know the difference between right and wrong. We can try to justify our actions or look to society's norms to validate our actions, convincing ourselves that what we've done or what we are doing is okay. But deep down we all know the truth and the truth will always surface at some point.

Also, there are so many things that can happen daily to each of us that are beyond our control because we live in a severely imperfect (sinful) world filled with severely imperfect (sinful) people. Our world is broken because we are unknowingly infected with this hidden disease of *Spiritual Cancer*. I can only say this because I was severely infected with it myself. The bad events in my life left me miserable, angry, depressed, bitter, resentful, fearful, jealous of others and in extreme cases, suicidal. I felt I deserved better and the more I felt this way, the worse things got. I woke up with a sick feeling every morning. The stress and anxiety were awful. I was dying on the inside. The feeling of despair and hopelessness was overwhelming at times.

What I didn't realize was no matter how hard I tried, I wasn't able to change things and fix them. I dove into self-help books, spoke with psychologists, psychiatrists, life coaches and even psychics. I watched seminars, tried to stay positive and live the 'good vibes only' life. Yet even after seeking help and trying to implement these mind-over-matter methods, I sadly realized they were only temporary fixes. The simple fact remained; I still had no control over the everyday circumstances that hit me. No matter how strong-minded and strong-willed I thought I was, life at times would get the best of me and I would inevitably feel defeated.

So I can honestly tell you this now; life does not have to be this way. It does not have to be difficult and a constant struggle. I write this today to stress to anyone and everyone that there is hope. No matter what your state is now, no matter what you're dealing with, and what you have been through, there is a cure. And I'm not talking about a quick or temporary fix, but an actual cure.

God does not take any of this *Spiritual Cancer* lightly. This is not the corrupt, unhappy, unsatisfied, hurting and broken world He intended it to be. His strongest desire is for us to get back to Him and live beautiful, peaceful, non-corrupt, non-stressful, non-materialistic lives. What parent wouldn't want only the best for their child? And only He can do that for each and every one of us. He wants us to get back to what really matters and what truly is important. And this COVID-19 pandemic has been a big wake-up call for all of us.

If your computer crashes, you take it to a computer guy to fix it. If your body is broken, you go to a doctor to fix it. If your car breaks down, you take it to a mechanic to fix it. Whatever is broken, you go to an expert for help, an expert who can fix it.

So what happens when your mental state-of-mind breaks and anxiety, stress or panic sets in, affecting your soul/spirit? The most important part of you—the part that makes you, you. The part that lives on forever, the part that is eternal. Why not go to an expert? The One who created you? Doesn't it make sense that the One who created you would also be the One who can fix you and help with your problems?

I'm writing to tell you there is a cure for this debilitating disease of *Spiritual Cancer* that unknowingly affects and infects your soul. The only remedy, the only cure for *Spiritual Cancer* is to switch your focus from the problem to the problem solver and His name is Jesus. Amid all this doom and gloom, there is someone who is real, who is listening, and who is waiting patiently for you to invite Him into your life. He gives life to the lifeless and hope to the hopeless. He and He alone can fill that missing piece, or void within each of us.

Things like money, success, drugs, sex or alcohol are all just band-aids to mask the emptiness we are all feeling. None of these things and no other human, can fix the root of our problems—but He can.

We receive this cure through faith in The Greatest Physician of all—Jesus. The cure is complete removal of this *Spiritual Cancer* (sin) that is eating us alive: past, present and future. In 1 John 1:7 it says, "But if we are living in the light, as God is in the light, then we have fellowship with each other, and the blood of Jesus, his Son, cleanses us from all sin."

And it's easy to receive the cure; all you have to do is ask. Matthew 7:7-8 tells us, "Keep on asking, and you will receive what you ask for. Keep on seeking, and you will find. Keep on knocking, and the door will be opened to you. For everyone who asks, receives. Everyone who seeks, finds. And to everyone who knocks, the door will be opened." God does not force Himself upon us or force us to believe in Him. Though He could, He chooses not to because He is a gentleman. True love is not demanded or forced. Even though you may love someone with all your heart, mind and soul, one fact remains; you cannot force anyone to love you in return. It is their choice to love you or not. And God is no different. He does the same by giving each of us free will.

However, God did not design humans to live apart from Him. As a father and mother are to their child, He is the one who created us, and He loves us immensely. When we choose to believe in God, we can hold tight to His promises. Eternity in Heaven. Jesus Himself conquered death and was resurrected. As followers of Christ, we too will be resurrected after death and are promised an eternity in Heaven. For it is then, that life really begins. Our human bodies, our shells will disintegrate back into the dust of the ground, but it is our soul that will live on forever. What does all this mean?

Jesus lovingly revealed to humanity that although we are imperfect (sinners), His love for us was so deep and immeasurable that He constructed a perfect plan. He willingly left His heavenly throne, became human, and accepted the sacrificial punishment for our sin on our behalf. Jesus did not come to earth to save the saints (the ones who try to appear perfect); rather, He came for the sinners (the ones who are imperfect and aren't afraid of admitting so). Sound crazy?

Perhaps, but look at it this way. How many loving fathers and mothers would gladly trade places with their beloved child who is fighting for their life in the cancer ward of a hospital if they could? How many parents would willingly sacrifice their own lives to save their child? The same is true with our Heavenly Father.

The Bible says the reason we would love God is because He loved us first. Jesus willingly died in our place in order to bridge the gap between sinful humanity and a Holy God. Jesus' sacrifice was the only way for us to enter into a relationship with God. Now and forever. Of all the religions known to humanity, only through Jesus will you see a God that reaches out toward humanity and because of His love for us, provides a way for us to have a relationship with Him. Jesus is living proof of a divine heart of love, meeting our needs and drawing us to Himself. Because of Jesus' death and resurrection, He offers us a new life today. We can be forgiven, fully accepted by God, and genuinely loved by Him. This is our God in action.

Take it from someone who was completely against organized religion, church and even the mere mention of God. I wanted no part of any of it. Churches to me, were filled with a bunch of brainwashers, manipulators, fake people and hypocrites who seemed more concerned with taking my money. I was clear in thinking that there was no God. And if there was a God, I thought he was mean and evil. And why would anyone believe in someone or something they cannot see? The entire premise of God was foreign and far-fetched to me and I looked at it as a crutch for weak-minded people to fall back on.

Well, I guess you could say He proved me wrong. But it wasn't until I was at the end of my rope and clearly desperate when I finally let my guard down and was open enough to trust and believe. As it says in Proverbs 3:5-6, "Trust in the LORD with all your heart; and lean not unto your own understanding. In all your ways acknowledge Him, and He shall direct your paths." God promises that only true blessings come from following Him. Because no other way can deliver what God promises. In fact, every other path delivers the exact opposite of what it promises.

Some of the most highly successful people in the world are actually the most unsatisfied because deep down they are restless, unhappy, and spiritually empty. And any attempt to self-medicate or use alternative methods will fall short, because what we are dealing with is a disease no one is exempt from and one which no human doctor can cure.

The key to life is realizing we cannot do it alone. We must come to the realization that we need help. Because we all do! I'll say it again, it doesn't matter who you are, what you've done, how much money you have, or don't have, how successful you are, where you were born, the color of your skin. None of that matters. Strip it all away and you will see we are all the same. We all suffer from the same ugly symptoms caused by life's daily struggles. And yet the most successful, wealthy person in the world and the poorest, most disadvantaged person in the world have equal access to the greatest gift life offers: a cure for all emotional pain and suffering. And the best part of all, this gift is free.

Sure, you may be going through a time or season in your life where things are going well; when life is great, and you have no complaints. But things will change. There is a constant flow of good and bad all the time. Such is the imperfect world we live in. It's completely unavoidable. Unexpected, sometimes devastating things can happen to us in an instant. This COVID-19 pandemic is a perfect example! Or it could be a car accident, news of the loss of a loved-one, losing your job, the list goes on.

Problems are unavoidable. They are woven into the very fabric of daily life in this fallen world. Our habitual response is to immediately go into problem-solving mode, and yet this separates us from God. When we can't solve our problems, we become discouraged, and the root of discouragement is unbelief. Discouragement blinds our eyes to the mercy of God and makes us perceive unfavorable circumstances.

We will never be able to counterattack discouragement on our own unless we turn to God, believing that He loves us, wants only the best for us, and trust whole-heartedly that He is in control. We are so limited in our capacity to fix what is wrong that it is in our best interest to talk with God about whatever is on our mind, seeking His perspective in every situation.

He masterfully crafted our minds to be in constant communication with Him. He listens and hears all our thoughts. He wants us to bring Him all our fears, hopes, needs and desires. Psalm 37:4 says, "Take delight in the LORD, and he will give you the desires of your heart." He designed us to commit everything into His care and turn from the path of grinding, planning and controlling, to the path of peace. He did not design the human mind to figure out the future. He designed us to relax, stay calm and trust Him with our future.

I'm not going to say asking for help and trusting God is an easy thing to do, because it's not, and it's a continual process. Asking for help may be perceived as a sign of weakness. It's a form of surrendering control of your life and that is one of the hardest things I personally have ever done and is the hardest thing for any of us to do. I still have days where my humanness kicks-in and I instinctively try to take control of a situation again and again. Or I start to worry or stress about things in the past or future—especially when it comes to a seemingly bad decision I've made.

I even questioned writing this book. Did I truly believe what I was writing? Was I being a hypocrite? What I didn't realize then, but fully understand now, is there is a very real 'enemy' that is lurking out there that continually attacks our minds and thoughts daily (I will elaborate more on this subject in a later chapter). But there were days when this 'enemy' would attack my thoughts so hard that I was convinced everything I had written was untrue. For weeks at a time I would walk away from writing, believing the lies the enemy was planting in my head. But then I (or God) would give myself a good, swift kick in the pants and remind myself of the truth —who I am and who I belong to and how He has radically changed my life for the better.

As I mentioned in a previous chapter and whether you choose to accept it or not, every detail of our lives is under God's control. Everything, including the bad, fits into a pattern for good. Many people believe that things happen by chance or occur randomly by coincidence. When we view the world this way, we have overlooked one simple little fact: the limitation of human understanding. Even before I knew God, I always had a basic understanding that things happened for a reason.

I remember a time when I got into my car and drove several blocks down the street before realizing I forgot my cell phone.

Somewhat annoyed, I turned my car around and drove back home to get it. I finally started back on my way and as I passed by the place where I had just turned around, I noticed up ahead there was a huge car accident. I immediately thought to myself, "Had I not turned around and gone back for my phone, that car accident could have involved me!"

Have you ever considered how often God is working behind the scenes to protect us from potentially bad things that we're not even aware of? It is important to be thankful in all situations, because you never know how many mishaps or accidents God has protected us from, without us even knowing. What we know and see of this world is merely scratching the surface. Submerged beneath the surface of the visible world are mysteries too vast for our minds to comprehend. If only we could see how He is constantly working on our behalf, then we would never have any doubts of His existence.

The lesson here is, we must learn to accept each moment as it comes, no matter how bad or good the circumstances may be and remember that God is sovereign over our lives. Instead of worrying, resenting, or regretting situations, we must turn our thoughts toward God and trust Him. Philippians 4:6-7 tells us, "Don't worry about anything; instead, pray about everything. Tell God what you need, and thank him for all he has done. Then you will experience God's peace, which exceeds anything we can understand. His peace will guard your hearts and minds."

So we should not be fearful, but instead give thanks to God and rest in His divine sovereignty. A thankful mindset keeps us in touch with God. The second we start to grumble, complain or worry, we are instinctively questioning our mighty Creator's sovereignty. Thankfulness in every situation is a safeguard against those yucky emotions. Gratitude enables us to see the light of His presence shining on ALL our circumstances.

I read a quote once that said, "Worry is like sitting in a rocking chair; it will give you something to do, but it won't get you anywhere." It is not so much adverse events that make us worry or anxious as it is our thoughts about those events. Our minds engage in efforts to take control of a situation in order to bring about our desired result. Our thoughts close in on the problem like a pack of ravenous wolves. Determined to make things go our way, we never even consider that God oversees our life. So the longer you starve yourself of God's presence in your life; the longer you allow *Spiritual Cancer* to eat you alive.

Spiritual Cancer, in the form of stress, anxiety, fear and worry has plagued the human race since the beginning of time; yet in these modern times with modern medicines and innovations, scientists and doctors have not found a cure.

But the cure is right in front of us. In Matthew 17:20, it tells us if we were to have just a small amount of faith, the size of a tiny little mustard seed, then nothing will be impossible. It just takes a tiny bit of blind faith and it's as simple as asking Him for help.

Just start with a small dialogue in your mind and admit to yourself and to Him, that you've made some mistakes and need some help. He already knows the truth anyway. Otherwise, unconfessed mistakes (sin) will lead to spiritual coldness, and deep down inside you will start to feel sick, depressed, uneasy, heavy, oppressed—and perhaps ashamed of what you may have done in the past. Afterall, we cannot turn back the hands of time and change something we've already done. Then sit back, relax, and watch what He can do.

Based on my life prior, compared to my life now, here's what I know: there is a complete cure for *Spiritual Cancer* and His name is Jesus. He is ready, willing and able to offer you the one thing you are looking for. Only He can fully satisfy. If you're skeptical, I understand. I myself would have never believed it until that night in India when He showed me—deleting all my past heartaches, worries, fears, regrets, guilt, and then filling me with His immense and undeniable love. He is the one who filled that the void within me—the one I had been longing to fill my entire life. The same void we are all born with.

I know it may sound crazy, strange, insane or weird, but all I can say is, it's the truth. And if what I've said can trigger just ONE of you to think for a second and give Him a chance, then sharing my crazy story was totally worth it. Because one thing remains. My best day without God, will never compare to my worst day now with God. Knowing that even in the worst of times, He's got my back. There is no greater comfort or confidence, and my desire is for each and every one of you to also experience Him. Jesus is the cure!

HIS PLANS ARE GREATER THAN OUR PLANS:

It was August 2008, five months after my text message from God, and it was time for our bi-annual equestrian tradeshow in Philadelphia, PA. I was still on such a 'God-high', that I would share my God story with anyone and everyone who would listen. As soon as I arrived to help set up our booth, I couldn't help but share the story with my colleagues about what had happened to me in India just five months prior. Not long before, I had that big falling out with my boss Timmy, when he referred to me as a 'nightmare' and refused to increase my monthly commission.

Well, after my God experience, I was in such a happy place, that I was able to put those negative feelings aside and join him, along with a few other colleagues for dinner that night after our booth set-up was complete. With a new set of ears, I began sharing my crazy God story once again. Timmy listened on and seemed a bit taken-aback to hear all that had happened at his farmhouse. I got to a point where I didn't even care how weird people thought I was for sharing such a crazy story. All I knew is it was the truth and I was filled with such excitement that I didn't care what anyone else thought.

Another three months went by and it was now November 2008. Timmy had flown from India and was visiting his warehouse in PA. He called me from the office and asked how I was doing. He asked if I received my commission check for the month and I told him I had. He said, "Really?" Again, I said, "Yes, it was for $400." He said, "You don't sound upset about this." I said, "No, why would I be?" I continued, "Don't you remember what I told you back in August at the tradeshow? I could be homeless, living on the side of the road with my daughter and be the happiest person in the world. I told you I finally found what I was looking for all my life and it was Jesus. It wasn't money that I needed. What I needed was love—and God provided me this abundantly. I am now the happiest and most content I have ever been and it's all because of Jesus."

Timmy shockingly replied, "Wow! I have never heard of or seen such a dramatic change in a person as I have seen in you. That is incredible." I agreed and said, "Yeah, I guess we won't be arguing over financial matters anymore." We both laughed.

That is when Timmy began to fall in love with the new person I had become. He had seen first-hand the dramatic change within me. A man who had grown up his entire life in India, entrenched in religious customs and rituals and surrounded by a world of self-help and meditation, and he had never seen a change, let alone such a dramatic change, in anyone. And that is one of the most obvious examples that sets Christianity apart—it's not just about a 'belief' in a higher power—rather, this higher power will transform your life.

He and I fought for years over financial issues, and now I was telling him how I could be homeless with my daughter, living on the side of a road and still be the happiest person in the world. It was a night and day difference, and this was mind-blowing to him. This change surely piqued his interest and regardless of all his material wealth and comforts, he wanted what I had. He was attracted to this peace and contentment I had found. He wasn't at all attracted to the old me, but he was instantly attracted to the new and improved me—Jesus within me.

As weeks went on, he constantly questioned and tested me to see if this new-found peace and contentment was just a temporary thing. But as months went on and he saw that the change in me was real and permanent. That is when Timmy's own personal journey with Jesus began.

Unbeknownst to us both, God not only had planned for Timmy to buy my business, but He had an even bigger plan and purpose beyond that. That boss of mine, Timmy, is now my life-long partner, not only in business but in marriage. God had clearly orchestrated this from the beginning. Yup, that's right. The woman he said must be a nightmare to be married to (yours truly!) is now his wife. I remember asking him on our wedding night, "So how does it feel to be married to your nightmare?" It will always be our longest running joke.

I often think back to a life-defining conversation Timmy and I had in the fall of 2006. It was my first trip to India, and I had just given birth to my daughter a few months prior. So as a new mom, I was overwhelmed with those motherly hormones and emotions. One day, Timmy and I had left the factory to grab lunch. As we were leaving the restaurant, two small children came running up to me.

The younger one, less than 2 years old was completely naked and the older one, maybe 3 years old, just had a dirty t-shirt on. The youngest one wrapped his tiny little body around my leg, which stopped me in my tracks. I looked down at this sweet little boy and tears were flowing down his face. He looked up at me with his big brown eyes and in that moment, I too started to cry as I looked at Timmy and said, "What is this?" Timmy gruffly said, "Come on, just get in the car." I looked around, hoping to find a parent but there was no one in sight. I said, "We can't just leave them here."

Timmy, growing up in India his entire life, was completely numb to all this as he frankly replied, "There's nothing we can do."

My heart was broken. As tears continued to stream down my face, I slowly made my way to the car. I closed the door and turned to Timmy and said, "There must be something you can do about this." He laughed and said, "What am I supposed to do? What can one person do?" I said, "All it takes is one pebble dropped in a body of water to cause the ripple effect. Someday I will be that pebble," I said.

Little did I know, less than four years later, that pebble would drop. It happened after a Sunday luncheon we hosted outside of New Delhi for our 1200 employees and their children. I spent the entire day just loving on all the beautiful children and their families. It was a bitter-sweet day, knowing that the kids would soon be going back to their villages, with little hope for their future. After everyone was gone, Timmy turned to me and said, "I know what we're going to do. We are going to start a free school and educate these children." Doesn't quite sound like the same, numb and emotionless Timmy from a few years ago does it?

Overwhelmed by the idea, I welled up with tears and gave him the biggest hug. Just three weeks later, we came across a small school building to lease (as if it was dropped right into our laps) and our mission was set in motion with just 45 students. Salvation Tree School was born.

Never in a million years did Timmy and I think we would be founders of a school in India. We were apparel manufacturers who knew nothing about education. Not to mention a school so large now, that it can accommodate nearly 2000 students. But in 2010, God planted a vision and passion within our hearts, and we were merely His hands and feet. We often step back and think, "How on earth did we do this and why on such a large scale?" But the answer is easy. Only with God. And we have countless stories of how He led and guided us every step of the way. We were never alone.

Words cannot even explain the pure joy we feel as we see our students flourishing. And none of this would have been possible without such an incredible God who also provided us with an incredible God-honoring principal and staff. So when Timmy and I start to feel the weight of the financial burden and debt we have incurred from this overwhelming venture; it is instantly forgotten when we experience the gratitude and love from our students and their parents. There truly is nothing greater. And if it's God's will and plan for us, we will continue to build more Salvation Tree Schools throughout all of India.

As the Bible says, "It is more Blessed to give than to receive." This could not be a truer statement. And it is our strong, unwavering faith that ensures us, without a shadow of a doubt, that He will continue to guide and provide. He always has and He always will. And as I think back on the series of events that lead to where we are now, there is a perfect scripture I am reminded of in Isaiah 55:8-9, "My thoughts are nothing like your thoughts,' says the LORD. 'And my ways are far beyond anything you could imagine. For just as the heavens are higher than the earth, so my ways are higher than your ways and my thoughts higher than your thoughts.'"

I've had some friends back home tell me they would never want to be Christian because life wouldn't be fun anymore. They said they didn't want to live by a set of rules. I get it. Who wants to live by a set of rules? I remember when I was a kid, I hated rules. Just hearing the word 'rules', made me instinctively want to rebel. But now that I'm a parent myself, I understand why my parents had rules. Because they loved me. And the reason I have certain rules for my daughter is because I love her, want what is best for her and I want to protect her to the best of my ability.

Just think about some basic rules we live by daily, like the rules of the road; what side of the road we drive on, obeying traffic signals, or stopping at stop signs, or the more obvious rules like not killing one another, not stealing, or not physically or sexually abusing someone. Rules clearly are not a bad thing when we look at them in this context and understand that they are put in place to protect ourselves (either emotionally or physically) as well as others.

So I'm not exactly sure which of the Christian rules my friends were referring to when they said life would no longer be fun. Because it is quite the contrary. I can confirm that my life now with God is way more fun and exciting than it ever was before! First and foremost, I would have never married Timmy, we would have never started our school in India, and I definitely would have never been half the mother I am now for my daughter. After reading the Bible, I have learned Godly standards and attributes that I have thankfully been able to pass on to her throughout her life. As I mentioned previously, I was not a shining example of a teenager or even a grown woman. I was never taught these Godly principles and instead, had a negative opinion of God. I was a hot mess. So it's obvious that God deserves all the credit now, for transforming me into the woman I am today; so that I could be the wife and mother He intended me to be.

It's difficult enough raising children and making sure, especially a single child, doesn't become spoiled. I have taught her to be loving, kind, respectful, appreciative and compassionate toward everyone. And to always see the best in people and to build them up with her words. She has been traveling to India with us since she was 3 years old. She has seen and been surrounded by extreme poverty. She doesn't take anything for granted. She has grown up alongside her two best friends in India, Anjali and Nidhi, who have been going to our school since the very beginning. I have taught her to always help others and put other people first. To not speak negatively about people and to never think she is better than anyone. Afterall, we are all created equal.

And most importantly, her relationship with God has given her such inner peace, strength and confidence, knowing that no matter what, God will always be there for her and protect her, even when I, or her Papi aren't around. She has learned, from a very young age, that when she prays and asks Him for help, He is always there. I remember it started with just simple little toddler prayers when she needed help finding a doll, a toy, or headphones. Within minutes she would find them in some random, unlikely place, and she'd excitedly give God the credit. Or now when she prays before a test, or a soccer game, or for her friends. Whatever it is, big or small, He has NEVER let her down. Those were the simple, yet profound building blocks that God established with her from a very young age. Now that is priceless! And it's as simple as that. All we have to do is have the faith of a child and see for ourselves. We just need to give Him the chance.

My life did a complete 180 since becoming Christian. I can honestly say, there is nothing more exciting than knowing that an All-mighty, All-powerful God has an awesome plan for my life. I now have this deep-rooted joy and confidence that I never had before, and I see life through a whole new set of eyes. As if I was seeing life before through a dull, black and white lens and now with God, I see through the brightest, most vibrant, multi-colored lens, giving me a whole new appreciation and perspective.

Think about how exciting it would be if someone told you to pack your bags because they had a huge surprise for you. All you knew is you would be getting on a plane and flying somewhere, but you just didn't know where. Now perhaps you are one of those people that doesn't like surprises and you'd prefer to plan ahead. But just pretend for a moment—pretend you had no other responsibilities and you could just let everything go, without a care in the world. Just hop on that plane and go. Just imagine how fun and exciting it would be! And that is exactly what life is like with God.

So now it's your turn! Start praying about that dream you have! That is the first, simple step to acting on it. Pray about it and watch how God will guide you. It's these small, simple steps, done with consistency and done with intention that will draw you closer to Him. You will see Him start to work in your life. But you have to act on it. Some people may never act on their dreams because of fear —fear of the unknown. And before they know it, years go by and they never did anything because they were afraid. But I am here to tell you; do not be afraid, do not be nervous and do not worry about the outcome. God has it all figured out for you.

Albert Einstein once said, "A ship in harbor is safe, but that is not what a ship is built for." We too were not made to live a life that is safe or meaningless. We all were made for so much more. More than our minds can even fathom. God has planted dreams, visions and passions within each of us and we must push aside our fears and take the first step with confidence, knowing He will provide everything we need to accomplish our dreams. King David confirms this and wrote this powerful message in Psalm 23:1-4, "The LORD is my shepherd, I lack nothing. He makes me lie down in green pastures, he leads me beside quiet waters, he refreshes my soul. He guides me along the right paths for his name's sake. Even though I walk through the darkest valley, I will fear no evil, for you are with me; your rod and your staff, they comfort me."

Doors of opportunity may start to open, and some doors may close, which is okay because this is how we are redirected. Be careful not to get discouraged and don't expect God to wave a magic wand and say, "Waalah! Here's your request!" It doesn't quite work that way. Sometimes you will be amazed at how quickly your prayers are answered, but more often than not, you may feel like your request has fallen on deaf ears. When this is happening, rest assured He has heard you, and know that often when there is a delay, He is most likely refining your character through the process. The only way to gain character in a certain area is to go through the very circumstances that build it. Character is not a gift or something we are instinctively born with, it's a learned skill that needs to be developed. One of the biggest jokes in Christian circles is to never pray and ask God for more patience. Unless you truly want it. And I mean truly. Because boy will He answer that prayer and then some. Just be prepared to sit back and be frustrated and annoyed like never before. Patience can only develop when your patience is truly tested.

But the most exciting part of this relationship with God is the new-found confidence you will have, knowing there isn't a step you can take that will be outside of God's perfect will and plan for your life. There are no more mistakes or accidents. So even when bad things happen now, you will be able to see and recognize them as merely speed bumps, slowing you down only for a bit, as you take a step back to see what is to be learned in the situation. He promises to be with you, every step of the way, so just stay focused on the big picture and continue on with confidence. Proverbs 16:9 tells us: "We can make our plans, but the LORD determines our steps."

Chapter 11

RELIGION vs. RELATIONSHIP

So if I still have your attention, and you don't think I'm completely cray-cray, then let's get down to the nitty-gritty. I live in Wellington, Florida, and compete show jumping at the Winter Equestrian Festival held here each year. Bill Gates' daughter also rides horses and competes here. While walking to my next event, I once overheard one person telling another, "I have Bill Gates' cell number. I just spoke with him the other day." I guess most people would think this was a pretty big deal. But as I walked along, I smiled to myself and thought, "You may have a direct line to Bill Gates, but I have a direct line to the One who created Bill Gates." Boom!

In Jesus' time, Jewish leaders perverted God's Law into a works-based religion that alienated people from God Himself. However, the law did serve a purpose. The Ten Commandments, for example, were given to us by God for our benefit and to show us how innately corrupt people are. Otherwise, how would we know? These commandments (God's Divine Law) were not meant to condemn us, rather, they were given to point out how imperfect humanity is.

So the law is a good thing. It reveals to us that we are imperfect, that we make mistakes and these mistakes separate us from a perfect and Holy God, which in turn, highlights our need for a Savior. People may assume the Ten Commandments are ancient and outdated, when they actually hold a practical value in this world. Can you imagine what society would be like without these principles?

Most of these same principles are still enforced by our legal system. So clearly they cannot be that ancient or outdated.

But where the Spiritual Leaders (Pharisees) of Jesus' time went wrong, was they prided themselves on their ability to keep the Law—at least outwardly—and lorded their authority over the common people who could never keep such strenuous rules. The Pharisees obedience to God's law was an attempt to earn salvation. And as great as they were at rule-keeping, they failed to recognize God in the flesh (Jesus) when He was standing right in front of them. They were so entrenched in rituals that they chose religion over a relationship. As said in Romans 3:20, "For no one can ever be made right with God by doing what the law commands. The law simply shows us how sinful we are."

Just as the Jewish leaders made a religion out of a relationship with God, people do the same with Christianity, specifically in creating rules not found in the Bible. Some who profess to follow Christ are actually following a man-made religion in the name of Jesus. While claiming to believe Scripture, they are often plagued with fear, guilt and doubt that they may not be good enough or that God will not accept them if they don't perform to a certain standard. This is religion masquerading as Christianity. And God does not take this lightly.

We all have this notion that Jesus walked the earth as a passive guy. But that is a big misconception. We must not mistake His kindness for weakness. I apologize in advance if what I'm about to say offends you; but let the truth be told—Jesus was the original badass. And I say this with the utmost love and respect. He came to do what no other had ever done before—set the record straight and tell it like it is. He was a vessel of truth. He certainly did not mince his words and He was not afraid to stand up for the truth and call a spade a spade. You can clearly see Jesus' true character as he addresses the crowds regarding the religious leaders at the time, here in Matthew 23:5-9, "Everything they do is for show. On their arms they wear extra wide prayer boxes with Scripture verses inside, and they wear robes with extra-long tassels. And they love to sit at the head table at banquets and in the seats of honor in the synagogues. They love to receive respectful greetings as they walk in the marketplaces, and to be called 'Rabbi.'"

He then turns to the religious leaders themselves and addresses them directly in Matthew 23:27-28, "What sorrow awaits you teachers of religious law and you Pharisees. Hypocrites! For you are like whitewashed tombs—beautiful on the outside but filled on the inside with dead people's bones and all sorts of impurity. Outwardly you look like righteous people, but inwardly your hearts are filled with hypocrisy and lawlessness."

During His time, Jesus did not like seeing these religious leaders and Pharisees exalting themselves above everyone else, and instead of pointing people to heaven, they were actually keeping people far from God. Jesus then continued boldly by calling them hypocrites and saying that everything they did was done for show and that on the inside, they were filled with dead people's bones. Holiness and obedience to Scripture are important, but the religious leaders were missing the point. Love was the difference. Jesus came to love and show love to all, while they were all fixated on self-righteousness, exalting themselves, judging others, and following a list of rules.

Unfortunately, we have seen the proof of this today with all the disturbing sexual allegations that have surfaced within the churches. There are thousands of cases where the so-called religious men and/or leaders today, have been accused of sexually abusing women and children. For years these accusations have been swept under a rug and the actual evidence and claims against them have been destroyed. This is beyond unacceptable. Do these men truly believe they are above the law?

I watched an interview with a woman, now in her 60's, who explained a time when she was sick in a hospital for several weeks when she was ten years old. While she was there, a priest would come to visit her daily. She then tells of how his daily visits turned into night-time visits. He then started to touch her inappropriately, take nude photos of her which made her uncomfortable and then he started having intercourse with her. One night she boldly spoke up and told him to stop and that what he was doing was wrong. He then had the audacity to say to her, "But I am a holy man and God lives in me, so how can I, as God Himself, be doing anything wrong?" He continued, "If anyone is bad here, it is you." For many years she believed what he told her and blamed herself.

Until later in life, and after much counseling, she finally realized that none of it was her fault. She then found out that she was not alone. She was not the only victim and in fact, there have now been several accounts of these supposed holy men within the church who were doing this same thing to others. That is when she began to fight back against the hypocrisy. It's disturbing and unacceptable to hear of any person sexually molesting a woman or child, but in my opinion, it seems a thousand times worse when it is done within the church, a supposed safe and holy place. This is exactly what gives God, Christianity and the church a bad name.

So here is where Christianity is radically different from all other religions: Christianity is based solely on a relationship with God through His son Jesus. The roles here are reversed: God Himself is the initiator, and man is the beneficiary. In Romans 8:3 it says, "The law of Moses was unable to save us because of the weakness of our sinful nature. So God did what the law could not do. He sent his own Son in a body like the bodies we sinners have. And in that body God declared an end to sin's control over us by giving his Son as a sacrifice for our sins."

Embracing Christianity is not about signing up for a religion, it's about entering into a relationship. Just as an adopted child has no power to create an adoption, we have no power to join the family of God by our own efforts. We can only accept His open invitation to know Him as a Father through HIS adoption of us.

God's sacrifice is the relationship that God has established with His children. The Bible states in Romans 3:23 that there is nothing any person can do to make themselves right with God, "For everyone has sinned; we all fall short of God's glorious standard."

We ALL fall short: which explains why humanity will suffer throughout our lives and is the entire point as to why Jesus (God in human form) came to earth to set the record straight.

We all wrestle with unrighteous thoughts and actions. We are all tempted to make bad choices. We struggle with greed and the desire for more and more. We find joy in gossiping and slandering—

as if it makes us feel better when we talk poorly about others. And the list goes on.

But the good news is; we don't need to clean up our acts and try to be perfect, or alcohol-free, sex-free, drug-free or even stress-free to begin this relationship. It is a non-judgmental 'come-as-you-are' relationship. It is not for any of us to judge anyone else's actions or behaviors. It is strictly between each individual person and God and is the basis of the relationship I am talking about—minus the religion. And the best part is, there are no ground rules for how we enter into this relationship and there certainly is no discrimination against race, color, creed, ethnicity, sexual orientation, economic status, gender or age.

The bottom line is, God does not discriminate, nor should we. We are all created equal. He created us ALL in His image. One of the most well-known Bible verses is John 3:16, "For God so loved the world that he gave his one and only Son, that whoever believes in him shall not perish but have eternal life." And there we have the answer, once and for all, to the longstanding debate as to who God loves. It says God loves the world, which includes everyone in it. There are no ground rules and there is no discrimination.

Tim Tebow is well-known not only for being a Heisman trophy winner, but as a strong Christian, you may also remember him for boldly writing this John 3:16 verse under his eyes before each of his football games. What an amazing platform he has been blessed with to spread this message. One of the most powerful verses of all—Jesus came and died for all of us—the entire human race. And it is His desire for us all to love Him in return. So no one, including Christians, should pass judgement on anyone. That is God's position and His alone. And He offers this free gift to everyone and anyone.

A very dear friend of my husband and I happens to be one of the funniest men we've ever met. We truly love this man. Not only is he an intelligent businessman, but the way he can make us laugh is like no other. One day we were chatting and somehow my Bible Study came up in conversation and he proceeded to call me a 'Jesus Freak'. Now, this certainly did not offend me because I actually love being called this. To me, it is an honor. But he then continued saying a few other things with a slightly 'judgy' tone. I finally stopped him in his tracks and said, "You know how much I love you right?" He replied, "Of course." I continued, "Well I don't make 'judgy' comments about you being gay do I?" He replied, "No." I said, "Well then I'd appreciate it if you would not judge me or make comments about the fact that I love Jesus." He looked at me like a deer in headlights and said, "Wow, I'm so sorry, I didn't even realize…"

I will never forget the wise words of my dear, sweet mother-in-law, Priti Sharma, who sadly and recently left this world. She used to say, be careful pointing a finger at someone, because there will always be three more pointing back at you. And such is the plight of the 'double-standard' and judgment amongst each other. The simple solution is found in Matthew 7:1-3, "Do not judge, or you too will be judged. For in the same way you judge others, you will be judged, and with the measure you use, it will be measured to you. "Why do you look at the speck of sawdust in your brother's eye and pay no attention to the plank in your own eye?"

Proverbs 18:21 also tells us "The tongue has the power of life and death…" One of the smallest organs in the body yet the most power-ful. We can either build each other up with our words or tear each other down. We all must be careful and be aware of our words, be-cause it is far too easy for any of us to fall into the trap of judging or gossiping and not even realize it.

You may or may not have, at some point in your life, heard of the Apostle Paul from the Bible. Paul was one of those Pharisee's I mentioned previously, who despised Christians and purposefully made it his life's mission to persecute and murder Christ followers. That is, until he had one of the greatest Christian conversions of all time. God used Paul mightily throughout his lifetime to write the majority of books in the New Testament. Paul too was a broken man who could humbly admit he wasn't perfect. He bore the weaknesses of his own sin and struggled against them continually, and he was very open and honest in sharing his struggles with others. Here is what Paul says in Romans 7:14-25,

Struggling with Sin

"So the trouble is not with the law, for it is spiritual and good. The trouble is with me, for I am all too human, a slave to sin. I don't really understand myself, for I want to do what is right, but I don't do it. Instead, I do what I hate. But if I know that what I am doing is wrong, this shows that I agree that the law is good. So I am not the one doing wrong; it is sin living in me that does it. And I know that nothing good lives in me, that is, in my sinful nature. I want to do what is right, but I can't. I want to do what is good, but I don't. I don't want to do what is wrong, but I do it anyway. But if I do what I don't want to do, I am not really the one doing wrong; it is sin living in me that does it. I have discovered this principle of life—that when I want to do what is right, I inevitably do what is wrong. I love God's law with all my heart. But there is another power within me that is at war with my mind. This power makes me a slave to the sin that is still within me. Oh, what a miserable person I am! Who will free me from this life that is dominated by sin and death? Thank God! The answer is in Jesus Christ our Lord. So you see how it is: In my mind I really want to obey God's law, but because of my sinful nature I am a slave to sin."

In 2 Corinthians 12:8-10, we then see Paul begging and pleading with God, not just once but three times, to take away this sin, which he refers to as a 'thorn'. "Three different times I begged the Lord to take it away. Each time he said, "My grace is all you need. My power works best in weakness."

Wow. That must have been surprising to hear but literally music to Paul's ears—I know it was music to my ears! And should be music to all our ears. I'll be the first to admit, we will continue to live imperfect lives (sin), whether we continually worry, stress, get angry, give in to temptation, whatever it is, but God Himself tells us His grace is enough—His power is made stronger in our weakness. Paul then continues on and says: "So now I am glad to boast about my weaknesses, so that the power of Christ can work through me. That's why I take pleasure in my weaknesses, and in the insults, hardships, persecutions, and troubles that I suffer for Christ. For when I am weak, then I am strong."

We are not surprising God with the choices we make, because it is He who gives us free will. He gives us freedom and authority to make our own choices, but it is the humble recognition of our broken condition that can turn us back to the grace of God. He's already aware of our imperfections, which is why He came to earth to do what He did for us. He intentionally came to earth because of the deep love He has for each of us and then willingly did what no other has done before.

He did for us what we cannot do for ourselves, as stated in 2 Corinthians 5:21, "For God made Christ, who never sinned, to be the offering for our sin, so that we could be made right with God through Christ." We cannot fix ourselves. Our only hope lies in this grace-based relationship between us and God, which illustrates the foundation of Christianity and the antithesis of religion. Feeling or believing you are a 'good' person just isn't enough. I stress again; there is nothing any of us can do here on earth that will ever be good enough to enter into this relationship with God. He graciously offers us this free gift and it is up to us (since He has given us free will) to accept it or not.

Remember in grade school when you'd line up for gym class and the teacher would pick two captains, and each captain would then start picking their own teams? Typically, they would be told to pick a girl, then a boy, and so on. How awesome did it feel to be chosen? You felt a sort of warm and fuzzy feeling inside, right? It sure is a wonderful feeling to be accepted. It's an even better feeling to be chosen.

Of all the millions of other people out there, your spouse or your boyfriend/girlfriend chose you. Now take that thought to the Nth degree, times a billion. God, the same God who created the entire universe, has chosen you to be adopted into His family here on earth and then to join Him in glorious heaven for eternity. It's mind-blowing to even think about. There truly is no greater honor.

So the ball is in your court. He has already extended His hand to all of humanity. We just need to do our part—reach up and grab it. And it's easy to start this relationship with a simple dialog in your head, which believe it or not, is a form of prayer. It doesn't have to be anything fancy and you don't have to worry about saying the right or wrong words. You don't need to sit in a church or even talk to a priest. This is between you and God alone. No one else needs to hear or even know. While people in Italy were confined to their homes due to the Coronavirus outbreak, they were upset because they weren't able to confess their sins to a priest. So the Pope himself released a statement saying everyone should speak to God directly. And that goes for all of us. Just come clean with yourself and with Him. He hears your thoughts anyway and already knows the ins and outs of your life. So nothing you say or ask for will surprise Him. Just admit you've made mistakes and/or need some help. It's that simple.

Then, you may begin to see certain signs, or you could receive an obvious answer to your prayer which are all the beginning stages of your relationship with God. And just like any other relationship, it will take time. So be patient. Think about the beginning stages of any new relationship. You talk on the phone, meet for coffee, lunch or dinner, you go places together, you spend time getting to know one another. And the more time you spend with someone, the better you get to know them. The same is true with Jesus. So just keep those lines of communication in your head going. Don't give up. Trust me; the life-long benefits of this relationship will be well worth it.

Because when you accept Jesus into your life, it is the greatest gift of all and here is what He promises in John 14:15-17, "If you love me, obey my commandments. And I will ask the Father, and he will give you another Advocate, who will never leave you. He is the Holy Spirit, who leads into all truth. The world cannot receive him, because it isn't looking for him and doesn't recognize him. But you know him, because he lives with you now (referring to Himself) and later will be in you (the Holy Spirit was released into the world after Jesus was crucified and raised from the dead)."

We are then given an Advocate: The Holy Spirit. Advocate means helper. So the Spirit within us will act as a guide, a teacher, and a helper, so we no longer have to do life alone. The Holy Spirit comes to live inside our hearts. He does not ask us to try to attain holiness by our own strength, as religion does. We merely need to surrender our old ways of thinking and acting so that His power can live through us.

At that moment, we are made new; we are 'born again'. Our old selves are gone (our past, our wrongdoings, our shortcomings, everything) and a new life begins for us as is promised in John 1:12-13, "But as many as received Him, to them He gave the right to become children of God, even to those who believe in His name, who were born, not of blood nor of the will of the flesh nor of the will of man, but of God." Born again of God. We basically die to our old selves and are given the greatest gift of all—a brand new and improved life!

I understand the term 'born-again' is a tough one to grasp. If you recall, I was also severely opposed to the term. It wasn't until I fully understood it's meaning when I could wrap my brain around it.

In the following verses, a religious leader named Nicodemus was also confused and asked Jesus to explain in John 3:1-7, "There was a man named Nicodemus, a Jewish religious leader who was a Pharisee. After dark one evening, he came to speak with Jesus. "Rabbi," he said, "we all know that God has sent you to teach us. Your miraculous signs are evidence that God is with you." Jesus replied, "I tell you the truth, unless you are born again, you cannot see the Kingdom of God." "What do you mean?" exclaimed Nicodemus. "How can an old man go back into his mother's womb and be born again?" Jesus replied, "I assure you, no one can enter the Kingdom of God without being born of water and the Spirit. Humans can reproduce only human life, but the Holy Spirit gives birth to spiritual life. So don't be surprised when I say, 'You must be born again.'"

God's original plan was for man to be an eternal being, but Original Sin, the sin we bear from birth, brought death to the spirit. That part of us created to comprehend and have fellowship with God, is dead at our births as is noted in Romans 6:23, "For the wages of sin is death, but the gift of God is eternal life in Christ Jesus our Lord."

Our physical bodies have come to life at birth as we breathe our first breath of air, but our spirits have not come to life yet. The term 'born-again' is not birth as we understand it. It basically means our souls come alive (or are 'born-again') when the Holy Spirit takes up residence within our hearts. Little did I know that at the age of 37, I would actually refer to myself as 'born-again'.

I never even wanted to be around those born-again crazies, let alone be personally known as one! I had an awful opinion of them—clearly based on my narrow-minded, judgmental (sinful) mind. My only experience with born-again Christians was when they'd come up to me and say, "If you don't accept Jesus Christ as your Lord and Savior, you are going to spend eternity in Hell." Great opening line, right? Who on earth wants to hear that? And probably not the best way to approach a non-believer.

So as crazy and far-fetched as this 'born-again' thing may sound, all I can say is, it's the truth and there is nothing better. I am living it daily and you can too. Because of God's great love for us, His desire is for us all to know Him, to draw near to Him, to pray to Him, to ask for His help, His guidance, and to love Him in return. 1 John 4:16 says, "And so we know and rely on the love God has for us. God is love. Whoever lives in love lives in God, and God in them.

❖ TRINITY ❖

I'm sure you've noticed by now that I use the name of God and Jesus interchangeably. It's important to know that God is comprised of the Father, the Son and the Holy Spirit which is referred to as the Trinity. God embodies all three—all are one in the same and all have existed before time. John 1:1-2, In the beginning was the Word, and the Word was with God, and the Word was God. He was with God in the beginning." God the Father planned to come to life in human form and His name was Jesus. In other words, Jesus was God. He was the living proof and the living word of God. John 1:14, "The Word became flesh and made his dwelling among us. We have seen his glory, the glory of the one and only Son, who came from the Father, full of grace and truth." Then, when Jesus willingly died on the cross, was sacrificed for our sins, and was raised from the dead, the Holy Spirit (also of God) was released into the world to dwell within the hearts of all who choose to believe. It is God's Holy Spirit that guides us and helps us to live better, more enjoyable lives—it molds and develops us to be more like Him—to think as God thinks and to do His good work. John 14:16-17, "And I will ask the Father, and he will give you another Advocate, who will never leave you. He is the Holy Spirit, who leads into all truth..."

The Trinity paints a beautiful picture of relationship and also shows the role of complete equality within a relationship. Just as the Father, Son, and Holy Spirit are of equal importance and are all fully God,

> they do function in different roles within their relationship.
> The Trinity teaches us we are all created equal and that people
> need other people—we were not meant to do life alone.
> We were designed to live within community and to have meaningful
> and loving relationships not only with other humans but also with God.
> It is God's greatest desire and our internal yearning,
> to reconcile this relationship.

Again, this is not about religion; it's about a relationship. In life, we will all continue to face impossible situations—ones that are totally beyond our control. This awareness of our inadequacy is not something we should ignore, and it is precisely where God wants us to be—and the best place to encounter Him and His glory and power. When you see armies of problems marching toward you, all you need to do is cry out to Him (either silently or aloud) and allow Him to fight for you. Then just sit back and watch as He works on your behalf.

It's all about having trust and being educated. Learning the foundation of truth versus what our own thoughts and perceptions are. To be 'born-again' is to be embraced by God. It's placing your faith and trust in the One who strongly desires to stand with you. Being 'born-again' means taking a good, honest look at yourself and admitting and accepting your imperfections (sins).

It is our human nature to be prideful and feel like we're in control and can handle every situation that comes our way. It's only when we humble ourselves, accept what little control we do have, and admit we are not 'all that' when we can experience a new life. It's only when we get to this point that the Spirit of God can then do its mighty work of transforming our lives.

Just like a caterpillar climbs into a tree, wraps itself in a silky robe, goes to sleep, and emerges a butterfly; we too can come by faith to Christ and emerge a new person. This may sound crazy, but it is precisely what happens. As it is written in 2 Corinthians 5:17-19, "This means that anyone who belongs to Christ has become a new person. The old life is gone; a new life has begun!"

Keep in mind, even when we are 'born-again', we all will continue to sin (make mistakes). No matter what. As I have said, we are all born this way. But what we can do now is turn to God, confess our sins (by simply admitting we've screwed up), and He will forgive us. It's that simple. His forgiveness literally lifts the burden of guilt from us. We are free and cured of this *Spiritual Cancer*. And we now have a lifetime of do-overs, because He has now recreated us with a new slate and unlimited chances. But don't take this the wrong way. This certainly is not a free pass for us to do whatever we want, whenever we want, just because we will be forgiven. Rather, we will experience a heightened sense of awareness with the Holy Spirit living within us (more powerful than our conscience) and this will, gradually change our thought processes and our actions as we are transformed into a new and improved person.

We will act in love. Love will become our dominant emotion. We will be prompted to apologize and ask for forgiveness from people we have hurt. We begin to make wiser choices, wiser decisions, we have a heightened sense of clarity in any and all situations. We will begin to see others as God sees them—through the lens of love. This love enables us to show compassion, empathy, kindness, understanding and be non-judgmental toward others. The Holy Spirit will guide us with positive emotions and protect us from the ugly, negative emotions brought about by the *Spiritual Cancer* that eats away at us. We will experience a new-found confidence and peace, all while receiving His supernatural guidance and direction. Call me crazy, but who wouldn't want this? Isn't it everyone's desire to be a better spouse, parent, friend, co-worker and just a better overall person?

Sure, we can try, in our own strength, to learn how to take control of every aspect of our lives and try to live stress-free. However, we will most likely come up short with the ever-changing events that surround us daily. Having complete control of our lives is like chasing the wind, it's just not possible. If it were, most of us would be able to do it. We might be able to change for a certain amount a time, but chances are, it will not last.

So my question is, "Why work so darn hard when the quick, simple and easy fix is right there in front of all of us?" None of us have the power to change things on our own. The simplest, easiest thing to do is ask the One who can change things for the better.

By its nature, sin (our imperfections) especially in the form of pride, keeps us spiritually blind and is why we cannot admit we are sinful and the number one reason why we may not want to accept this invitation. This is the exact reason why Jesus came to preach 'recovery of sight to the blind'. Time and time again it is mentioned throughout the Bible that Jesus performed many miracles to prove to the people that He was who He said He was. He brought people back from the dead, He healed lepers, He healed people plagued with a disease or a disability, He restored hearing to the deaf and restored sight to the blind.

Restoring sight to the blind was one of the more interesting miracles because not only was this a physical healing but Jesus also uses it as a metaphor for spiritual healing. *John*, chapter 9 describes a man who was blind from birth. He begged Jesus to give him eyes to see and Jesus granted him this. In that moment, not only were his physical eyes restored, but also the eyes of his soul. He was both physically and spiritually blind and once his physical eyes were opened, his spiritual eyes were also opened, and he immediately had faith and could 'see' that Jesus was God. Then the man was questioned by the Pharisees about Jesus' healing and the man responded John 9:23, "...All I know, I was blind but now I see!"

We have all seen a glass window, door or windshield that becomes dirty over time. Perhaps due to salt, sand, rain or snow. Or even dirty little fingers that leave prints on the glass, inhibiting our ability to see through it clearly. But with a paper towel and some cleaning solution, all those dirty marks can be wiped clean, revealing crystal clear visibility as if the glass were brand new again. This is exactly the same cleansing God does within our lives. We will continue to tarnish ourselves with daily dirt and fingerprints (sin), but through the power of the Holy Spirit, God similarly cleanses us of this daily dirt and grime (sin) and we are made new again—back to our clean, original state. The way God created us to be from the beginning.

It may surprise you, because it sure surprised me; the number of celebrities in Hollywood who speak openly about their relationship with God. Jim Caviezel, among other roles, played Jesus Christ in Mel Gibson's, *Passion of the Christ*, the seventh highest-grossing-film to date in the US. Caviezel is a hugely passionate Christ follower.

We all know the funny and super-spunky, singer, songwriter, actress and former TV Host, Kathie Lee Gifford. I just love her and how bold and outspoken she is about her faith! Tyler Perry, best known for his *Madea* movies, is hilarious and one of my favorites. When interviewed, he is not shy about mentioning the importance of faith in his life.

Mark Wahlberg refers to his relationship with God as the most important part of his life. In an interview with Anthony Pearce for *Squaremile.com* he is quoted as saying, "I pray every day... My faith in God is what makes me a better man," he says, earnestly. "It's the most important part of my life. I pray that I will live up to my intention to be the best husband and father that I can be. I never would have been able to change my life and have the success and love that I have in my world today without my faith."

I absolutely adore Roma Downey, from the show "Touched by an Angel" and her husband, famed producer Mark Burnett who have inspired many with their projects like "The Bible," "A.D.", as well as many other faith-focused feature films and TV shows.

We all know the popular TV Host Steve Harvey, especially from Family Feud. He credits God for his success and in an interview with Essence magazine, Harvey's wife Marjorie explained, "Our relationship with God is the centerpiece for love in our family."

One of my favorite actors Chris Pratt is very vocal about his faith. Pratt has taken the stage at a couple of award shows and has made his love for God known. At the 2018, *MTV Movie & TV Awards* he encouraged teens and young adults to look beyond them-selves by saying, "God is real. God loves you. God wants the best for you."

Dwayne Johnson (The Rock) made a career out of pro wrestling that eventually led to his success as an actor. He admits he has a special relationship with God that has helped him through depression, among other struggles, and he counts his blessings daily.

In a recent interview, one of the greatest actors of all time, Denzel Washington, the two-time Academy Award winner said, "I'm here to serve God."

Oscar-nominated Angela Basset is proud of her relationship with Christ. She is well-known for her strong female roles, which she says were formed, at least in part, from her faith.

Carrie Underwood, a successful singer, song-writer, fashion designer, and actress has never kept her faith a secret and almost always mentions her faith in interviews. She sings one of my personal favorites, "Jesus, Take the Wheel."

Kirk Cameron, best known for his role as Mike Seaver on the ABC sitcom *Growing Pains* and his sister Candace Cameron Bure who you'd remember for her role as D.J. Tanner on *Full House*, are both born-again Christians. Kirk has recently made several Christian-based movies and you can find his sister Candace starring in several Hallmark movies. She's not only an actress, but a producer, author, and talk show panelist.

After the tragic death of George Floyd, Emmanuel Acho, a former NFL linebacker now with FOX Sports, has emerged as one the most prominent voices for breaking down racial barriers, and promoting harmony while remaining centered in Christ. In an article written by Kevin Mercer for *SportsSpectrum.com*, Acho said his recent activity has ultimately been through God's strength and for God's glory. "There is often a difference between your career and your calling, and it's clear that God has led me to my calling over the last 10 days. I have been blessed to be a blessing and use my voice for the betterment of the world and the glory of God."

And there are many other well-known celebrities who are strong in their faith: Matthew McConaughey, Ryan Gosling, Nick Jonas, Demi Lovato, Patricia Heating, Mario Lopez, Dolly Parton, Todd Chrisley, Keith Urban, Kristin Chenoweth, Justin Bieber, Stephen Baldwin, Jack Brewer, EJ Gaines, Governor Mike Huckabee, Eric Metaxas, Brian 'Head' Welch and Reginald 'Fieldy' Arvizu from the Grammy award winning band Korn, and the list goes on.

One thing is for sure; no matter who you are, where you come from, or what you've done in the past, anyone who decides to enter into a relationship with Christ is adopted into the same family—God's family, where we are all connected as fellow brothers and sisters in Christ. And as children of God, our spirits come alive and we see life from an entirely new perspective.

We now know where we came from, why we are here, and where we are going. In the midst of a world living in spiritual darkness, we are lovingly invited into an intimate relationship with our Heavenly Father. One where we can be set free from the chains of sin—those ugly emotions that keep us in bondage and hold us captive, and instead, we can walk in freedom as a child of the light! John 8:34-36 says, "Jesus replied, "I tell you the truth, everyone who sins is a slave of sin. A slave is not a permanent member of the family, but a son is part of the family forever. So if the Son sets you free, you are truly free."

We no longer live in spiritual darkness and plagued with Spiritual Cancer. In John 8:12, Jesus spoke to the people once more and said, "I am the light of the world. Whoever follows me will never walk in darkness, but will have the light of life." It's Gods desire to share His mysteries with us and reveal the truth.

Chapter 12

SPIRITUAL WARFARE
THE HIDDEN BATTLE

Just as a heads-up, some of you may find this chapter a little unsettling or perhaps you may not believe evil even exists in this world. Either way, we have all seen that famous cartoon with a tiny little red devil holding a pitchfork sitting on one shoulder whispering into a person's left ear, and a small angel sitting on the opposite shoulder whispering into the person's right ear. Believe it or not, this cartoon imagery isn't as far-fetched as you may think.

There is a very real battle going on daily, behind the scenes, that most of us are completely unaware of. Call it what you will, but the truth is, evil does exist in this world. Take any school shooting incident in recent years. Invariably we hear there were warning signs from the shooter leading up to these events, but no one took them seriously. It seems some people just turned a blind eye. The event itself is evil, as are the circumstances leading up to the event.

In a previous chapter, I made reference to this invisible enemy known to most as Satan, whose name means 'adversary.' But first, allow me to explain the backstory. Originally, Satan's name was Lucifer, and he was one of God's angels. However, at some point, he became corrupt and turned rogue. In Ezekiel 28:17, God addresses Lucifer directly and says, "Your heart became proud on account of your beauty, and you corrupted your wisdom because of your splendor."

Lucifer apparently became so impressed with his own beauty, intelligence, power, and position, that he began to desire for himself the honor and glory that belonged to God alone. The sin that corrupted Lucifer was pride. This action represents the very beginning of sin in the universe—long before the fall of man with Adam and Eve. Sin originated in the free will of Lucifer in which, with full understanding of the issues involved, he chose to rebel against God, his Creator.

Lucifer was then rightfully judged by God. In Ezekiel 28:18 God goes on to say, "I threw you to the earth." As a result of this heinous sin against God, Lucifer was banished from living in heaven. He became corrupt, and his name changed from Lucifer (morning star) to Satan (adversary). So then the question remains; how do we know for sure that there is a spiritual realm if we cannot see it? Many people today do not want to deal with a world they cannot see, especially when the world we do see is hard enough to deal with.

But before we can discuss the spiritual battle, we must believe in the spiritual realm. We tend to act like a two-year-old child who closes their eyes and places a blanket over their head, believing that no one can see them because they cannot see anyone. Just because we cannot see the spiritual realm does not mean it is not there. Whenever God is at work in your life, you can be sure Satan will be on the attack. His main goal is to try to stop and distract us from whatever God is doing.

Isn't it ironic how the world today is filled with more distractions than ever with the internet and social media? People barely communicate anymore because we are so distracted with our cell phones. Keith Green, a Christian song writer, wrote, "I [Satan] used to have to sneak around. But now they just open their doors. No one's looking for my tricks because no one believes in me anymore."

Isn't that the truth! But believe it or not, we are all living in a very real, daily battle—a battle for our souls. The enemy is attacking like never before. This is unseen spiritual warfare. These everyday battles make up the smaller components of a much bigger picture. By definition, battles involve combat between two persons, between factions, between armies, and they consist of any type of extended struggle or controversy. In warfare, battles are fought on different fronts, for different reasons, and with varying degrees of intensity. The same is true in spiritual warfare. Our spiritual battles are real, even though we cannot physically see the attacker. But what we can do is educate ourselves on how the battles are fought, and how they impact our lives.

However, if we choose to ignore or not believe in the spiritual realm, the enemy wins, because we will find ourselves confused, frustrated, anxious, depressed, worried, angry, fearful, stressed and perhaps suicidal, because we are believing the lies the enemy is feeding us and refusing the peace that God promises us. The best defense is a strong offense. Educating ourselves about the spiritual realm is only half the battle. The other half requires us to be well equipped and it is God who will provide us everything we need to be victorious. He is our only refuge.

I must encourage everyone now, more than ever, to consider doing their part to help win this war against *Spiritual Cancer*. The enemy is having a field day as he's sitting back and watching our country coming apart at the seams. America is in the throes of this spiritual warfare and the obvious symptoms are the sickness, disease, anger, violence, burglaries, and unnecessary homicides surrounding us in the wake of this pandemic and the social and racial tension.

America is divided.

Black Lives absolutely do Matter and that issue must be addressed. But I'm confused as to how peaceful protests for George Floyd escalate into looting and violent destruction of buildings, cars and businesses. As well as harming and killing other people. How does that even make sense?

I understand there are some bad cops out there. But we all know there are always bad seeds in every bunch. Every company, school, sports team, business and even some of our families have bad seeds. Wherever there are groups of people, there will also be a few bad seeds. So we cannot group police officers together and judge them as a whole and assume they are all bad. Isn't that the entire point of racism? To not judge a book by it's cover? No one has the right to judge anyone. Period. It's that same double-standard I mentioned previously, and two wrongs do not make a right.

But for sure, some form of questioning and testing must be implemented, within each police precinct, to weed out the bad and keep the good. I'm certainly not a scholar on the subject but what I do know is this— yes, there are problems within our country that need to be addressed. But problems are never solved with brute force, violence or by trying to cram our opinions down someone else's throat. The hate, anger and rage must stop and there is always a way to peacefully and intelligently solve any problem—no matter how difficult or how bad it gets.

Believe me, there's nothing worse than feeling defeated. Feeling broken and worn down. That empty feeling of hopelessness and despair can be overwhelming. Or that feeling of anger and hate that eats you alive. No one likes to feel this way. So why are we allowing these negative feelings to control us?

We all can take back our control by making a choice to break this dangerous cycle. Many of us have a desire to help make a change, and to contribute to a cause we believe in, but before we do this, we first need to look from within and start with ourselves. We can agree that none of us are perfect and we are all living with some form of this *Spiritual Cancer*—and we all need to be restored. We are all harboring and carrying baggage from our childhood and/or our past. So once we accept this and simply ask God for help, healing and forgiveness, then He can swoop in and start to do some spiritual house cleaning. Not only will we begin to feel better, but our healing will then positively influence and affect everyone around us.

As contagious as this Coronavirus is, this cleansing is just as contagious, but in a positive way. Your friends and families will start to see this positive change within you—that deep rooted peace and joy will be undeniable, and they will naturally want what you have and to experience the same for themselves. It only takes a spark to start a forest fire. We each need to be that spark within our families, amongst our friends and within our communities.

I must be honest. Once the decision is made to take this leap of faith, it doesn't mean life will immediately become easy and filled with unicorns and rainbows. Just know we will all continue to face opposition in this life. But rest assured, God has graciously provided spiritual tools and weapons to help us fight any and all battles we may face. We just need to understand that the battle is not against flesh and blood, but against powers in the spiritual world. And as we gain an understanding of this spiritual realm, we will begin to understand how the enemy moves against us in the physical realm. There will still be trials. In fact, Jesus promises that there will be trouble in the world. In John 16:33 He warns us, "I have told you this so that you may have peace in me. Here on earth you will have many trials and sorrows. But take heart, because I have overcome the world."

Jesus came and conquered our greatest fear and the worst thing possible—death. When Jesus died on the cross, Satan thought he had won by ending Jesus' life once and for all. But what Satan didn't realize is this was part of God's master plan. After three days, Jesus was resurrected, God raised Him from the dead and brought Him back to life. It is written in 1 Corinthians 15:3-8, that over 500 people, in addition to His twelve disciples, saw Jesus over a 40-day period after His resurrection (Acts 1:3), proving that when we die, God will also raise us (our souls) back to life as we spend eternity in Heaven with Him.

So now with Him by our side, we can conquer anything. There is nothing in this life, including death, that He did not come and endure, in order to help us overcome all our own personal fears, struggles, heartaches, and problems. Our circumstances may appear to be awful and devastating, but the gift of the Holy Spirit living within us will provide the supernatural peace and confidence we need during those circumstances. Bad circumstances are unavoidable because of the fallen world we live in. But Jesus came so that we can see this world through a new set of eyes: His eyes. And now we have more of an eternal perspective versus a worldly perspective. The goal here is for us to be clear-eyed and prepare properly for this battle.

The Bible doesn't tell us too much detail about Satan and how he works (because our focus is to be solely on God), but it does tell us two important truths about him. First, he is real—he does exist, and he will do everything in his power to draw us away from God. He will always tempt us to do what is wrong and to turn away from God. Second, and most important, the Bible tells us he is already defeated.

By Christ's death and resurrection, Jesus conquered Satan and won the battle.

So by the power of the Holy Spirit within us, we can boldly, firmly and confidently stand against him. Don't be deceived by Satan's lies when he tries to tell you, "God doesn't really exist; or you're not good enough; or sure, go ahead and take that drug, you'll be fine." It's that same voice that tempts us with things that might be bad for us: "It's okay, go ahead and get in the car; you've only had a couple of drinks." Or, "Go ahead and hook-up with your colleague. It's okay, your husband/wife will never find out." It is Satan's desire for us to be plagued with the hidden disease of *Spiritual Cancer*, just as he was with his own pride—and as the saying goes, 'misery loves company'.

One of the hardest battles on this earth is fought within ourselves. Sure, we may be able to understand and accept the truth of how the world lures and tempts us. But getting a grasp of what goes on within our own hearts and minds is the hardest, most exhausting battle of them all—and Satan just loves this. To begin to examine the battle within us, we must first understand its nature.

The desires of the flesh are part of our human nature, and its history goes back to the beginning of time as we know it. Have you ever felt that overwhelming desire within you to let sin be master over you? I know I have! We make decisions according to how we think, feel, and want and then we find ourselves struggling with the symptoms of *Spiritual Cancer* such as anger, bitterness, hatred, and lust, which inevitably leads us into areas of temptation.

But let's also look at the not-so-obvious examples of this spiritual warfare. Doubt is a perfect example. In a previous chapter, I mentioned having doubts about writing this book as well as doubts regarding the crazy dialogue I had with God in India. As time went on, the events became a distant memory. And the more I shared my story with others, the crazier and more far-fetched it began to sound, even to me. It was that little voice inside my head trying to convince me that none of it really happened, that it was all just a ridiculous dream. But amongst all the chatter and doubt I had going on in my head, one thing remained—my dialogue with Melanie. It was her knowing what I was going to say before I even said it—especially when it was about God. She always has been and always will be the validation I needed.

And even as I look back upon that moment in India when I was lying in bed and had myself convinced that Steve had kidnapped ParisElla, killed her and then killed himself; where did those fearful thoughts come from? Isn't it amazing what our minds can convince us of? Fear is another perfect example of the spiritual warfare going on around us and within us. Fear shocks us. Fear paralyzes us. It renders us unable to cope, unable to act.

It surely didn't make sense to me at the time, but looking back, it's no wonder the voice (God's voice) told me to 'tell them to leave, tell them they are not wanted here.' I now understand who He was referring to. The enemy's intent is to keep our eyes riveted on our fears and stop us from trusting God. To stop us from making wise decisions. To stop us from believing things can change. To stop us from pursuing the seemingly impossible dreams in our hearts.

John 8:44, says Satan is the father of lies. "He was a murderer from the beginning. He has always hated the truth, because there is no truth in him. When he lies, it is consistent with his character; for he is a liar and the father of lies." In John 10:10, Jesus tells us, "The enemy comes only to steal and kill and destroy." He then immediately offers us hope in the same sentence by saying, "I have come that they may have life, and have it to the full." And reminds us in Isaiah 41:10, "So do not fear, for I am with you; do not be dismayed, for I am your God. I will strengthen you and help you; I will uphold you with my righteous right hand."

Another common battle within us is the ugliness of unforgiveness. This is something we can all relate to. If someone has offended or wronged you, and I mean really wronged you, perhaps done the worst thing possible, it is almost impossible to feel like you can forgive them. We carry that anger, bitterness and resentment around with us like it's our best friend. However, I once heard that refusing to forgive, is like taking poison and hoping the other person will die. Unforgiveness will literally eat you alive and this is Satan's number one tactic, because all these negative emotions will keep us far, far away from the one main ingredient that connects us with God—love.

Instead of letting it go, we want that person to suffer and hurt, the way they hurt us. We desire for them to say they are sorry and when/if they do, we still are not fully satisfied. We want to yell and scream at them and make them suffer and blame them for our unhappiness. But the number one thing to remember is no matter what we say or do, we are not hurting them; we are hurting ourselves. It's our minds that play and replay what they did to us over and over again, like a broken record and we hold onto a list of offenses. We continually complain to others and we gossip about the person as if that's supposed to make us feel better.

This form of *Spiritual Cancer* is one of the worst, because it not only affects us emotionally and spiritually, but it affects us physically. When our emotional energy is drained, we lose good hormones like endorphins and dopamine and we feel sick, lifeless or depressed. The reality is, we are the one's suffering, not them.

Our Pastor, Craig Groeschel once said, "It's not about how much forgiveness a person deserves, rather, how much freedom you desire. Faith enables us to see an opportunity for freedom while those without faith, only see an offense." As strange as it may sound and as difficult as it may be, the only way for our own personal healing to begin, is to forgive the person who has wronged us. Forgiving doesn't mean forgetting and it certainly doesn't mean that we are to allow that person to continually hurt us. We are called to forgive and then we must build a safe boundary between ourselves and that person. This is one of the hardest things to do and we cannot do this on our own.

Some of us, at some point in our lives, have either heard or learned The Lord's Prayer. What I didn't realize, is this prayer actually came from Jesus' mouth and is written in the pages of the Bible. And one of the main points is forgiving others, as it is written in Matthew 6:6-15:

> "But when you pray, go into your room, close the door and pray to your Father, who is unseen. Then your Father, who sees what is done in secret, will reward you. And when you pray, do not keep on babbling like pagans, for they think they will be heard because of their many words. Do not be like

them, for your Father knows what you need before you ask him.

"This, then, is how you should pray:

"'Our Father in heaven, hallowed be your name, your kingdom come, your will be done, on earth as it is in heaven. Give us today our daily bread. And forgive us our sins, as we forgive those who sin against us. And lead us not into temptation, but deliver us from the evil one. For if you forgive other people when they sin against you, your heavenly Father will also forgive you. But if you do not forgive others their sins, your Father will not forgive your sins.'"

We see also in Ephesians 4:32 where it tells us to, "Be kind and compassionate to one another, forgiving each other, just as in Christ God forgave you." Jesus then takes it a step further and says in Matthew 5:43-44, "You have heard that it was said, 'Love your neighbor and hate your enemy.' But I tell you, love your enemies and pray for those who persecute you…" Love our enemies? Really? How are we supposed to do that?

The logical answer is—we cannot, in our own strength. We would never even consider this seemingly illogical action. But Jesus once again, leads by example and proves that with God's help, we all can do this.

Jesus, while hanging crucified on the cross, barely alive, cries out to God, His Father on behalf of his enemies, the ones who just brutally tortured him, and says in Luke 23:34, "Father, forgive them, for they do not know what they are doing." Jesus removed Himself from the equation and the circumstances leading up to His horrific beatings and crucifixion, and still cried out to God, His Father, to forgive them. And that is a perfect example of what we all must do. We may not have the power to forgive or to love and pray for our enemies in our own strength, but we can through God. And with His help, we are the ones that are set free from the bondage of hate and unforgiveness.

No matter what, we will continue to suffer in our flesh in this life, whether we feed its desires or deny its pleasures. We will constantly battle between what we want to do versus what we know is right. The Spirit of God brings us to life spiritually, yet we live in these bodies of flesh that still have a sinful nature. Thus, the battles will continue to rage even in the lives of believers—but victory is assured, because we have Christ on our side.

God equips us and helps us fight against our sinful feelings. But we must learn to recognize and fight against the very nature within us. The Apostle Paul tells us in Colossians 3:8-10, "But now you must put aside all such things as these: anger, rage, malice, slander, and filthy language from your mouth. Do not lie to one another, since you have taken off the old self with its practices, and have put on the new self, which is being renewed in knowledge in the image of its Creator." The Lord has given us His Spirit, who will empower us to overcome, but we must be willing to allow Him the authority to be in control of our emotions and behaviors.

So the good news is, the closer your relationship grows with Christ, the more protected and the farther away you will be from Satan. James 4:7-8 says, "Submit yourselves, then, to God. Resist the devil, and he will flee from you. Come near to God and he will come near to you."

A quick, simple way to know and recognize if the enemy is attacking is found in Galatians 5:22-23, "But the fruit of the Spirit is love, joy, peace, patience, kindness, goodness, faithfulness, gentleness, and self-control." So if you are feeling or experiencing anything other than those nine 'God-given fruits', then recognize and understand you are experiencing the negative forces brought on by the enemy. Feelings such as jealousy, fear, depression, stress, worry, insecurity, self-pity, shame, guilt, temptation, anger or disappointment. All these negative emotions come from the lies the enemy is feeding and bombarding you with. None of these align with our Holy Heavenly Father.

As we begin to recognize these negative emotions, the Bible tells us in 2 Corinthians 10:5, "...hold captive every thought and submit it to God". Because of my awareness now, I am getting better at putting this into action. The second a negative thought comes into my mind; I recognize it for the lie that it is, as I physically close my eyes, shake my head and say to myself, "Nope, I'm not going there!" and then I immediately turn my thoughts toward God. I no longer allow those negative thoughts to linger and take root. Instead, I nip them in the bud as soon as possible. The quicker we turn our thoughts toward God, the better we will begin to feel. So instead of struggling in our own strength and giving life to those negative emotions, it is so much easier to seek His help. It's only when we ask Him, that He mightily and miraculously steps in and fights our battles for us. How awesome is that!

No matter how much power and control of your mind and thoughts you think you have, none of us have the strength to fight against a supernatural enemy on our own. When our faith is strong, troubles become small. That doesn't mean troubles aren't real, or that they disappear. It just means we need help taking control of the enemy, instead of the enemy taking control of us. Just as Jesus triumphed over death, so He helps us triumph over our problems.

All we have to do is turn our focus toward God; knowing that He has not abandoned us, knowing He alone has the power to fight against this invisible enemy on our behalf and knowing that He has a purpose and a plan for our future through these battles. Jeremiah 29:11 says, "I know the plans I have for you . . . plans to prosper you and not harm you, plans to give you hope and a future." God is telling us He has a plan for each one of us, a plan that includes hope for the future. That is why we turn to our Mighty Creator to help us fight this supernatural enemy and fight fire with fire.

Jesus understood the temptations of the world. He knew that Satan would use every kind of enticement possible to lure people's hearts away from God. In the Book of Matthew, Chapter 4, Jesus was tempted three times by Satan. If Satan would try to lure Jesus Himself away from God, His Heavenly Father, clearly, he will try to lure us away as well.

Don't be surprised if the battle of spiritual warfare intensifies when a person decides to follow Jesus. The enemy will attack from all angles, hoping to dissuade the person from fully giving their heart to Jesus. He will use people, circumstances, events, fears and doubts in their minds to steal their heart back to his ways.

Jesus was well aware of this and warns us in Matthew 13:18-23 when he says:

"Now listen to the explanation of the parable about the farmer planting seeds: The seed that fell on the footpath represents those who hear the message about the Kingdom and don't understand it. Then the evil one comes and snatches away the seed that was planted in their hearts. The seed on the rocky soil represents those who hear the message and immediately receive it with joy. But since they don't have deep roots, they don't last long. They fall away as soon as they have problems or are persecuted for believing God's word. The seed that fell among the thorns represents those who hear God's word, but all too quickly the message is crowded out by the worries of this life and the lure of wealth, so no fruit is produced. The seed that fell on good soil represents those who truly hear and understand God's word and produce a harvest of thirty, sixty, or even a hundred times as much as had been planted!"

The seeds of a person's faith will either be sown on rocky soil, where it cannot firmly take root and will easily blow away when times get tough and the next big storm in life hits them, causing them to fall away. Or, the seeds that are sown in a person's heart will strengthen and take root on good, rich soil, when their heart is fully surrendered and confidently trusting in God and His ways. These types of battles are constantly being fought in the world and surely involve the spiritual forces of darkness that exist in the invisible realm around us. You can either hunker down and root yourself in strong, confident faith, or not. The choice is yours.

The good news I share is that we can all be conquerors. We can all be victorious and win this war. But it's not done by fighting with each other. It starts internally with us. We must each first, do our part and make a choice—as crazy, yet simple as it sounds, choosing God is the answer and will make us winners. I don't know about you, but I like to win. I really like to win, and it is my greatest desire for you and our entire country and the entire world, to win. One of my favorite sayings is: Put God first, and you will never be last.

Chapter 13

STRENGTHENING YOUR SPIRITUAL MUSCLES

Once a relationship with Jesus begins, it is then, and only then, that you will see and experience His supernatural hand in your life. I am constantly amazed at the overwhelming peace and strength He provides, especially in tough times. I am now able to see that nothing I face in this life will ever be too difficult, now that I have supernatural strength to turn to.

For most of my life, I never believed in God, so I completely understand the mindset of the atheists and all unbelievers. I believed religion was for the weak-minded people. The ones who were not strong enough on their own to get their lives together or the ones who needed some form of a crutch to get them through difficult times. Now I come across posts on social media where people question, belittle, or even attack God in the name of religion. And I totally get it, because I used to be one of them. I was the one who would mock and turn my nose up at the mere mention of God. I looked down on 'religious' people.

Afterall, isn't it the strong-minded and strong-willed people who succeed in this world? The ones who are driven and who work hard to attain success as they strive for excellence. The harder you work, the more successful you will be, right? This could very well be true for some of us, but would largely depend on each person's true measure of success.

What if, just for a moment, we were to analyze the converse? What if we flip our thoughts around and say that the ones who work hardest, who are the most successful, who appear to be in control of every aspect of their lives and don't believe in God, are actually the weaker ones? We're not talking physically weak, or even mentally weak, but perhaps spiritually weak. They could still be wildly successful based on society's norms, but spiritually they are weak. And why does this matter? Because it is the spirit that dwells within us that is the most important component. Our physical minds and bodies will disintegrate when we die, but our spirits live on forever. Our spirits are eternal.

The Bible teaches us that a person is more than just a body—each of us is a living soul. And our souls were created in the image of God. God Himself has implanted His own nature within each of us. Just as our bodies have certain characteristics and appetites, so do our souls. The characteristics of the soul include intelligence, emotions, and will. The human soul or spirit longs for peace, contentment, and joy. Most of all, the soul is longing for God—its yearning is to be reconciled to its Creator and to have fellowship with Him. That is the missing piece, or void within each of us.

We are constantly seeking ways to fill this void and, in our world today, we give most of our attention to satisfying the appetites of the body (which are the temporary fixes that leave us empty) and practically no attention to the soul. Consequently, we are one-dimensional. We become fat physically and materially, but spiritually we are lean, weak, and anemic. If we exercise and eat right, our bodies will be healthy and strong. If we pay attention in school, read, and study, then our minds will become strong. So why do we ignore our soul—the most important part of who we are? The soul demands as much attention as the body and in order to have the strength to fight our spiritual battles, the soul desires worship, quietness, and meditation (prayer) with our Creator in order to feed and rejuvenate itself.

For most of my life, I never even thought to ask God for help or turn to Him in my time of need, and because of this, I was never able to experience Him. It was only when I was truly desperate and had nowhere else to turn, when I finally turned my eyes toward Him and started to ask for help. Only then did He prove to me how real

He was by answering my prayers. Answered prayers are the building blocks to a strong faith. Once your faith is strong and rooted in the knowledge that God has a purpose and a plan for your life, then you will have supernatural confidence in any situation.

I have found three tried and tested steps that will definitely help strengthen your spiritual muscles.

❖ STEP ONE ❖

Step one is through prayer and/or meditation. This prayer doesn't have to be formal and you don't have to worry about saying the right or wrong thing. Prayer is as simple as the daily dialogue we think to ourselves in our heads. Whether you believe it or not, God knows your thoughts anyway. So whatever you are thinking right now in your head, I can assure you, He is aware. If you've made it this far into the book, I imagine He is absolutely thrilled because you are being open-minded and either knowingly or unknowingly searching for Him. His desire is for your heart and mind to seek Him and speak with Him which will open the door to your soul, allowing you to hear Him when He speaks to you.

I once had a conversation with a girlfriend who desperately needed money. She had a small boat she was trying to sell, and, after many months of trying to sell it, she had pretty much given up. I then asked her if she had prayed about it. She laughed and said, "Of course not!" I asked her why and she said, "Laurie, are you kidding me? God has much more important things to tend to. The last thing I'm going to do is bother Him with my stupid little request of selling my boat."

I then asked her if I could pray for her over the phone, she laughed and then agreed. After I finished praying, I told her, God doesn't care about what you are asking for; all He cares about is that you are turning to Him for help. Less than one week later my phone rang, and I saw it was her number. I answered the phone by saying, "Your boat sold didn't it?" She immediately exclaimed, "Yes! How did you know?" With a smile I said, "That's God for you!" I continued, "Prayer isn't about getting things you want, it's about giving God the opportunity to prove Himself real in your life."

When you entrust the details of your life to God, you will be pleasantly surprised at how thoroughly He answers your prayers. He takes pleasure in hearing your prayers, so feel free to bring Him all your requests. The more you pray, the more answers you can receive. Best of all, your faith will be strengthened each time you experience and witness how precisely He responds to your specific prayers. Because He is infinite in all His ways, you need not worry that He will run out of resources or that any prayer is too big or too small. So I encourage you to turn to Him, with open hands and hearts and be ready to receive all He has for you.

Before I became a believer, I was driving in my car, flipping through the radio stations when I came across a song with a catchy tune. I stopped and listened. Unbeknownst to me, it was a Christian song playing on the Christian radio station WAY-FM. I listened closely to the singer's words; "I love you more than the sun and the stars that I taught how to shine, you are mine and you shine for me too..." At that moment I was completely put-off as I wondered why a singer would be so arrogant and bold as to proclaim to have created the stars—and taught them to shine? Really? Who does this guy think he is? So I quickly changed the station.

A few days later I was flipping through the radio stations and came across that same song again. I couldn't help but listen more closely to the words and this time was different. As I continued listening, my eyes welled-up with tears as if a little light in my brain turned on and I had a strange realization that it was God speaking to me through those lyrics. I listened on; "I love you, yesterday and today and tomorrow, I'll say it again and again, I love you more..." The longer I listened, the more the lyrics penetrated my soul and pierced my heart. I remember that moment vividly as I later referred to that moment as one of my first 'God winks'.

My definition of a 'God wink' is an intense, emotional moment when I've been fully aware that God is right there with me, by my side, in that certain moment. As if He's saying, "I'm here with you, kiddo." My eyes and heart were opened to receive that message from Him at that very moment.

Matthew West is the man God chose to write and sing those lyrics to that song entitled "More". But in that moment, it was as if God Himself was singing to me. And that was one of the many signs He began showing me. We are all different, but I have found music to be one of the greatest ways to connect with God. I am now an avid listener of the Christian radio stations WAY-FM, K-LOVE and THE MESSAGE on SiriusXM. The music on these stations is so uplifting and family friendly and at the end of this book, I have made a list of songs that have impacted me the most. If you care to give them a listen, I believe you too will be amazed at how God can and will speak to you through music.

MUSICAL SIDE NOTE:

Prior to this, I had no idea Christian music even existed or that it would be cool enough for me to listen to. I know, how judgmental, right? Well, you might be as surprised as I was to know that there are Christian artists like Lauren Daigle whose music has crossed over into mainstream. She's won a ton of awards for her songs, some of which you may recognize: "How Can It Be", "You Say", "Look Up Child" or one of my favorites "First", as well as her newest release "Rescue". The combination of her strong, beautiful voice coupled with her even more powerful lyrics, are sure to pack a one-two punch to the depths of your soul.

Back in the mid-1990's, one of my favorite groups was called Jars of Clay. I first heard their song "Flood" on my favorite mainstream alternative music radio station. I liked the song so much that I bought their entire Album on CD. I loved every song on that CD and listened to it so much that the CD pretty much wore out! The songs and lyrics really resonated with me and it wasn't until many years later, after I became Christian, that I realized Jars of Clay was a Christian group singing Christian music! They were the first Christian cross-over band I had known of.

One of my personal favorites today is TobyMac. He's one of the top Christian music artists today. He was originally part of the band DC Talk, which was a successful Christian rock trio consisting of Toby McKeehan, Michael Tait, and Kevin Max Smith. DC Talk was hugely popular in the 1990's and won countless awards for their music. They became one of the first contemporary Christian groups to perform on late-night television on the *Tonight Show* with Jay Leno. One of their songs, "In The Light" is still to this day, our family favorite. The trio went their separate ways. Michael Tait became lead singer of the Newsboys in 2009, which is another one of my favorites. And TobyMac has had a hugely successful solo career.

TobyMac's songs to me, are the coolest, with their upbeat rhythms—incorporating rap, hip-hop and R & B styles combined with lyrics that are not only family friendly but speak to real-life situations. I highly recommend listening to any and all of his music.

Sadly enough, tragedy hit him and his wife not too long ago as they suddenly lost their 21-year-old son. He was their first-born and TobyMac just wrote and released a beautiful song tribute to him entitled "21 Years". It's a song that will surely resonate with anyone who has lost a loved one. No parent should have to bury their child and my deepest, heartfelt thoughts and prayers go out to him and his entire family.

In an Instagram post about his new song, TobyMac said:

" '21 years' is a song I wrote about the recent passing of my firstborn son, Truett Foster McKeehan," he says about this most personal song. "I loved him with all my heart. Until something in life hits you this hard, you never know how you will handle it. I am thankful that I have been surrounded by love, starting with God's and extending to community near and far that have walked with us and carried us every day. Writing this song felt like an honest confession of the questions, pain, anger, doubt, mercy and promise that describes the journey I'm probably only beginning. The rest is yet to come. One thing I know is that I am not alone. God didn't promise us a life of no pain or even tragic death, but He did promise He would never leave us or forsake us. And I'm holding dearly to that promise for my son as well as myself."

This is a devastating reminder that none of us are impervious to life's difficulties and tragedies, but as God tells us in Jeremiah 31:13, "...I will turn their mourning into joy. I will comfort them and exchange their sorrow for rejoicing." And we can also hold tight to the promise of Psalm 46:1, "God is our refuge and strength, always ready to help in times of trouble."

Then there are the musicians I bet you never knew were Christian. U2's Bono for one. I'm not sure if there ever has been or ever will be a more powerful band than U2. They have been my favorite band since I was a kid and I had no idea Bono was Christian. *VFN Kingdom Business* released an article on their website on January 1, 2019 saying, "Not too often does a lead singer of a rock band get to sit down with a Bible translator, but today that all changes. Eugene Peterson is the translator of *"The Message Bible,"* and he didn't know who U2's Bono was until he received a copy of a magazine. The magazine included an interview with Bono and that was just the beginning for Eugene to get to know more about Bono.

Bono starts the relationship by sending a video message to Eugene thanking him for The Message Bible translation and how it helped him and his band. "I wanted to video message you, my thanks and our thanks and the band for this remarkable work you have done. There have been some great translations and some very literary translations. No translation that I have read that speaks to me in my own language. So, I want to thank you for that..." The two have since filmed a wonderful documentary together, thanks to David Taylor, Brehm Texas, and Fourth Line Films, which can be found on YouTube, courtesy of Fuller Studio.

Many have heard of the band Lifehouse, with their songs: "Hanging by a Moment", "Broken" and the most moving songs of all time "From Where You Are" and "Everything". Lifehouse's music has probably impacted me more than any other. And for those who have seen the popular TV series *Grey's Anatomy*, I'm sure you'll recognize the song by The Fray, "How to Save a Life" which was used in many episodes. These are both well-known, mainstream rock bands. Neither classify themselves as Christian bands, but their lyrics and the band members themselves, have Christian roots.

We all know the beautiful model, songwriter, dancer and singer Ciara, with one of my favorite and most dance-worthy songs of all time; "Level Up", and her super-talented quarterback hubby of the Seattle Seahawks, Russell Wilson. After they began their relationship, Ciara said that she and Russell, a devout Christian, would abstain from having sex "until the deal is sealed," telling *E! News* that while it was a "great challenge" to remain celibate, it allowed them to continue to build their friendship." Ciara talked about the 'no premarital sex' policy in a recent interview with *InStyle*, published in its April 2019 issue. "That took a lot of prayer," the singer said. "It was hard. I can't lie."

And my husband, Timmy and I can also confirm—it truly is a difficult task, since we did the same. As a new Christian, not only did I want to honor God, but I remember walking down the aisle toward Timmy, knowing whole-heartedly I was marrying my best friend, and a man who truly loved and honored me for who I am and what I believed in, without the pre-marital sex blurring the lines.

And what about the super cool skater chic, Avril Levigne who is well-known for her pop-punk song "Sk8er Boi" as well as "I'm With You" and "Complicated". After a six-year gap, she released her sixth studio album in 2019, *Head Above Water*. The Title song, "Head Above Water" was released in 2018 and is described as "a powerful, spiritual epiphany detailing the Canadian singer's journey through her battle with Lyme disease." [15]

Avril was interviewed in the October 18, 2018 issue of *Billboard* by Anna Peele:

> "One night, in bed with her mother and barely able to breathe, Lavigne started to pray. "I had accepted that I was dying," she says. "And I felt in that moment like I was under water and drowning, and I was trying to come up to gasp for air. And literally under my breath, I was like, 'God, help me keep my head above the water.'" Lavigne grabbed her phone and opened Notes. She had the beginning of a song, and, if not a way out of the water, at least some light visible above the surface. The first time she sang it—or anything at all, after literal years—was at his studio. Lavigne was terrified. Would

her voice have withered, like her muscles? But when she opened her mouth, it was there. "God was like, 'Nope, you're going to keep doing music,'" says Lavigne. In that moment, she began to believe her gift was innate, holy and uncomplicated, now deepened into something more pro-found than her earlier expressions of frustration. "The silver lining of it"—making her way back to health after years of incapacitation and physical therapy and powerful drugs— "is that I've really had the time to be able to just be present, instead of being, like, a machine: studio, tour, studio, tour. This is the first break I've ever taken since I was 15." In this small way, Lavigne breaking was a blessing. And "Head Above Water" sounds like the prayer it is. And on the track, Lavigne's voice is huge, swollen with gratitude at its own existence, a whole chorus coming from one tiny body. "Music's powerful," says Lavigne and it is both surprising and perfect that she has a hit on the *Billboard* "Hot Christian Songs" chart.

❖ STEP TWO ❖

The second step for strengthening your spiritual muscles, comes from the spiritual food and nourishment we can receive from reading God's Word in the Bible. We all know how weak we become physically if we were to stop eating and exercising. But no one in their right mind would willingly do this. So why is it that we fail to see the connection between spiritual weakness and faith? Just like physical muscles, spiritual muscles do not grow automatically. They too require spiritual food, nourishment, and exercise. In *Matthew 4:4 "Jesus answered, "It is written: 'Man shall not live on bread alone, but on every word that comes from the mouth of God.'"* Not only is physical food necessary for us to survive, but also the spiritual food we receive by reading God's words in the Bible.

Nothing but God can ever completely satisfy, because our souls were made by God and for God. So we must not starve our souls. Instead, we must feed it and train it for battle. The Apostle Paul tells us in 1 Corinthians 9:24-27, "Don't you realize that in a race everyone runs, but only one person gets the prize? So run to win! All athletes are disciplined in their training. They do it to win a prize that will fade away, but we do it for an eternal prize. So I run with purpose in every step... I discipline my body like an athlete, training it to do what it should..."

Like an Olympic athlete who trains his body for competition, God wants us to train our minds in order to handle what may come our way—whether good or bad. The information found in the Bible will absolutely provide a solid defense against Satan's attacks.

This battle is addressed explicitly in Ephesians 6:10-17:

> "A final word: Be strong in the Lord and in his mighty power. Put on all of God's armor so that you will be able to stand firm against all strategies of the devil. For we are not fighting against flesh-and-blood enemies, but against evil rulers and authorities of the unseen world, against mighty powers in this dark world, and against evil spirits in the heavenly places. Therefore, put on every piece of God's armor so you will be able to resist the enemy in the time of evil. Then after the battle you will still be standing firm. Stand your ground, putting on the belt of truth and the body armor of God's righteousness. For shoes, put on the peace that comes from the Good News so that you will be fully prepared. In addition to all of these, hold up the shield of faith to stop the fiery arrows of the devil. Put on salvation as your helmet, and take the sword of the Spirit, which is the word of God."

For those of you who are put-off by the mere mention of the Bible, I can relate, because I was too. Afterall, isn't it an old, outdated book that only priests read? How could something written so long ago be relevant today? And what's the big deal anyway since it was written by some random people? And why are there so many different versions?

One of my preconceived notions about the Bible was that it was a book based on Holy, or 'perfect' people and could only be read by other Holy, or 'perfect' people. Let the truth be told, it is quite the contrary. It wasn't until I began reading through the pages myself when I realized it's a book recounting the lives of extremely imperfect (sinful) screw-ups just like you and me! And how God's redemptive love not only hand-selected each screw-up, but then used each one to perform the mightiest and most important of tasks.

Starting with Noah. We all know the famous story of Noah who God told to build the ark. Well that same Noah had a bad drinking problem and was basically labeled an alcoholic.

Moses, one of the greatest men of all time, met God up-close and personal in the burning bush and literally told God, He must have the wrong person. Moses didn't believe that he could be of any use to God because he had a speech impediment which made him hugely insecure. However, God assured Moses he was a chosen one and Moses had the honor, above anyone else, of speaking directly with God. He also led the Jews out of Egypt and out of slavery, he parted the Red Sea and was handed the Ten Commandments directly from God. Not too shabby!

Elijah, one of the greatest prophets in the Old Testament suffered from severe depression and was suicidal. Jacob, the son of Isaac, was a cheater and a liar. Joseph was mocked, abused and left for dead by his own brothers, sold into slavery, was wrongly accused of sexually assaulting his masters' wife and was then thrown in jail for many years. Surprisingly, Joseph kept his faith in God throughout and once released from jail, he became second in command to Pharaoh and was able to save his entire kingdom and his family during a time of famine.

Job, one of the wealthiest and most successful men of his time, had everything taken away from him. All ten of his children died in a house fire, he lost all his livestock, he lost all his wealth and then he himself was struck with a deadly illness. Literally everything was stripped from him. And although Job questioned God and wondered why these terrible things were happening, he held onto his deep-rooted faith and he continued to trust God despite all these numerous tragedies. Even just one of those tragic events would be enough to cause any normal person to question their faith. But because of his strong, unwavering faith, God not only restored his health, but blessed him with another 10 children and twice the amount of wealth he had prior.

We all know David, the brave little boy who killed Goliath the giant, with a sling shot and a stone. As he grew up, God chose him (the youngest and least likely of all his brothers) to be King. He is known as the apple of God's eye. But then, once he was King, David, with all his power, forced a married woman to sleep with him while her husband was away at war. She became pregnant with King David's child and he then ordered the woman's husband to be murdered during battle. David was an adulterer and a murderer who, saddened by his bad decisions, repented of his sins, showed sincere remorse and begged God for forgiveness. After suffering some pretty severe consequences for his very bad choices, God graciously granted David forgiveness and continued to shower him with blessings throughout his lifetime.

After Jesus was arrested, Peter, one of Jesus' favorite disciples was recognized by three different people and when they questioned him, Peter lied to each and denied even knowing Jesus.

Judas, another one of Jesus' disciples, betrayed Him by selling his whereabouts to the Pharisees for a small sum of money, so they could have him arrested and then killed. This betrayal haunted Judas so much that he ended up committing suicide.

Rahab was a prostitute who lived in Jericho in the Promised Land. She assisted the Israelites in capturing the city by hiding two spies in her home who had been sent to plan their attack. God then protected her and everyone in her family when Jericho was destroyed. One woman's faith changed an entire family's destiny.

There are many other stories about some less-than-perfect candidates that God hand-selected. But it is the Apostle Paul who gets the award for the 'least likely candidate' to be chosen by God to do His work. I mentioned Paul briefly in a previous chapter for writing the majority of books in the New Testament.

Soon after Jesus was crucified, Saul (whose name was later changed to Paul) was a Pharisee who, as I mentioned before, despised Christians and made it his life's mission to persecute and murder any and all of Jesus' followers. And ironically, I have to ask myself, how was I any different than Paul? How are any of us different from Paul? Clearly, we are not going around murdering Christians today, but we certainly may look down on them, judge them, speak poorly of them or perhaps think less of them. Either way, I think many of us have the propensity to persecute them in our thoughts, or by our speech or actions, don't we? I know I used to.

It wasn't until one particular mission where Paul was traveling with his team of men on the road to Damascus with plans to persecute more Christ followers, when his life dramatically changed, as described in the book of Acts 9: 1-9:

> "Meanwhile, Saul was still breathing out murderous threats against the Lord's disciples. He went to the high priest and asked him for letters to the synagogues in Damascus, so that if he found any there who belonged to the Way, whether men or women, he might take them as prisoners to Jerusalem. As he neared Damascus on his journey, suddenly a light from heaven flashed around him. He fell to the ground and heard a voice say to him, "Saul, Saul, why do you persecute me?" "Who are you, Lord?" Saul asked. "I am Jesus, whom you are persecuting," he replied. "Now get up and go into the city, and you will be told what you must do." The men traveling with Saul stood there speechless; they heard the sound but did not see anyone. Saul got up from the ground, but when he opened his eyes he could see nothing. So they led him by the hand into Damascus. For three days he was blind, and did not eat or drink anything."

Here again we see Jesus using the metaphor of both physical and spiritual blindness. After the third day, Paul's site was restored, and he then saw the world through a new set of eyes. As the saying goes, once he was blind and now, he can see. Not only was his physical sight restored, but now also his spiritual sight. After this dramatic incident, Saul's name was then changed to Paul and he was instantly trans-formed into a believer. He then spent the rest of his life traveling the world sharing the Good News of Jesus. And to this day, it is Paul who is the most well-known Apostle of all time.

Time and time again, the Bible shares accounts of how God hand-picked the least likely candidate to be the most useful and successful. The one's who either felt unworthy, the one's others overlooked, or the ones who appeared to be the least likely candidates. God sees the potential. They may not have exuded the outward appearance of strength, but God weighed their characters and saw their spiritual strength.

Now that I've hopefully explained the Bible enough to make it a little less intimidating; what if I told you that the Bible might just be the rulebook of life? Have you ever wondered why there was never a class in school on how to navigate through life? Or through marriage? Or through parenting? These are some of the most important issues in our lifetime, yet why is it we were never taught how to handle these very important issues?

The Bible literally teaches us and explains how to navigate through all of life's most important issues and more. It is one of our greatest gifts from God. His sole purpose for having it written is to lovingly teach us how to navigate through life. He does not want us to suffer and struggle. Although we cannot avoid the difficulties of this life, God promises and assures us throughout the pages, that He loves us unconditionally and He will always be there, by our sides, to help us through every difficult situation.

Just for the record, I personally have always hated reading and had never read one book from cover to cover until the Bible. Don't' ask me how I graduated college without doing this, but I somehow managed. Thank goodness for Cliffs Notes! So clearly the Bible is captivating enough to keep even my attention. And I must say that it has vividly helped me and taught me so much in my life.

And although the Bible was written several thousand years ago, God's Word remains the same. As it says in Isaiah 40:8, "The grass withers and the flowers fade, but the word of our God stands forever." Unlike your mobile phone, your television, your computer or your car, the Bible never needs an upgrade.

People often question why there are so many different versions of the Bible. The simple answer is because over time, the English language changed and evolved. For example, one of the oldest versions is known as The King James Version (KJV). This version is written using Old English words and terms such as 'thou art', or 'sayeth'. None of which are used in today's Modern English. So, over the years as the English language started to change, so did the versions of the Bible.

But let it be known, that even though there are many different versions, the overall message remains the same throughout. None of the Bible versions differ in the overall message. I own several different versions myself and I can confirm, some passages may use slightly different words, in perhaps a slightly different order, but the overall message in each is the same. My first Bible was The New Living Translation (NLT) version. I personally feel this version is the easiest to understand and would highly recommend this version for all first-time readers. And if you want to take it a step further, you can get an NLT study Bible. Within each chapter, there are written explanations which go into more explicit details to describe the overall message of each chapter.

And with wonderful technology today, there are some great free Bible Apps available to download on your phone. Perfect for everyone's on-the-go lives. There are many different apps available, and I will mention three of my personal favorites in the final chapter.

So here's what we know, we know God didn't sit with a pen and paper, jot down some thoughts and then toss down the pages of the Bible from His heavenly throne, but what He did do is what He still does today. He hand-picks ready, willing and able men and women to be His hands and feet. As it is written in 2 Timothy 3:16-17, "All scripture is inspired by God and is useful to teach us what is true and to make us realize what is wrong in our lives. It corrects us when we are wrong and teaches us to do what is right. God uses it to prepare and equip his people to do every good work."

He selected each person to write each of the books of the Bible and to share His message. In a way, it's similar to what I have done by writing this book; but on a much, much smaller and vastly inferior scale. *Spiritual Cancer* certainly wasn't my idea nor my doing since I was, and still am the ultimate screw-up and quite honestly, the least likely candidate. So I can't even take credit for it.

And I apologize if you've spotted some spelling, grammatical or punctuation errors within my writing since I'm not a professional writer, nor did I ever envision myself as one. I know my writing isn't perfect, but as long as the overall message and point gets across, then that's all that matters. And besides, I think it's better to find beauty within the imperfections, since that is the main theme of this book anyway.

In 2017, I was scrolling through Facebook one day when I came across a post of a very dear friend of mine, Jaimie Dahl. She announced she had been diagnosed with breast cancer and began undergoing treatments. She documented her journey on Facebook and the more I read, the more her story touched my heart and penetrated my soul. Then one day, God prompted me to start writing. As if He was dropping His own thoughts into my mind, I was just being obedient and writing them down.

One page led to another, and another and before I knew it, it appeared there was a full-fledged book in front of me. I look back now and see that all the trials, tribulations and heartache I endured throughout my life, were stories God purposely gifted me with for this very reason—to add life and credibility to this book. My life now is so exciting and fulfilling because of Him, that I want everyone to experience the same. Once I saw and experienced first-hand how real He is, it was easy for me to turn to Him, trust Him and allow Him to guide me in His will for my life. God is the true author of *Spiritual Cancer* and I was merely the one He chose to do the typing.

It was my friend Jaimie's story that God used to grab my attention and ignite that spark within me. Nothing happens by chance or coincidence and you just never know when God is going to work in your life. And I am so very happy to say that Jaimie's story was a beautiful and successful God story as her body is now free and clear of the cancer that could have taken her life. She too has written a beautiful book entitled *I Have Two Words For You: A story of one woman's journey to healing, freedom and faith.*

❖ STEP THREE ❖

The third step to strengthening your spiritual muscles is to surround yourself with like-minded people/believers. One of the greatest gifts God gives us is the gift of family, friendship and fellow-ship. As I mentioned previously, God did not create us to live alone. He created us to exist in groups and to have fellowship. I heard Pastor Levi Lusko once say, "We were created for connection, not isolation." As it says in Proverbs 27:17, "As iron sharpens iron, so one person sharpens another." It is best to surround yourself with those who can help guide you, give wise, Godly advice and be an overall good influence in your life.

A good place to find like-minded people is in a solid, bible-based church. There are so many fantastic churches out there and a lot can be found online. My husband and I found the best local church for us in our hometown of Wellington, FL called LifeChurch. The founder and senior pastor is Craig Groeschel and if you are so inclined, I highly recommend listening to his sermons online at *Life.Church*, or at one of the thirty-four (and growing) LifeChurch campus locations nationwide. This is where we have made some of our closest friends, including the campus Pastor Brian, his wife Jenni and their beautiful children.

Being there provides us an amazing support group. It's where we are fed the word of God from the Bible, and it's where our faith grows, and our spiritual muscles are strengthened. Pastor Craig's messages are always practical and ironically poignant to whatever circumstances we seem to be dealing with at any given time in our lives. As if God Himself is speaking to us directly, it's always the exact message we need to hear in that moment.

And what makes it even better, is how much our daughter loves it. I grew up dreading going to church. On the occasional Sunday, my mom would take my sisters and I to a very boring, very somber church and it was just awful. I would bite, kick, scratch and scream so I wouldn't have to go. So the fact that our teenage daughter loves going to this church with us is huge. She will bring friends along with her and they love it as well. I cannot explain it other than when you walk in, you feel alive. The atmosphere is welcoming, joyful, vibrant and exciting. There are no false pretenses, nor do you feel judged. LifeChurch has evolved for the changing times and let's be honest, if a church can impress and captivate teenagers, to the point they look forward to going back week after week, then they must be doing something right!

Joining a Bible Study or Life Group is another great way to strengthen your spiritual muscles. I was at a friends' 40th Birthday party and as the night rolled on, I can honestly admit I had a couple drinks in me. So with that said, I am quite bold about sharing my faith with people at any given moment anyway, but give me a couple drinks and I become even more loud and proud. That's just me.

> SIDE NOTE: Dare I say, at the risk of being judged, that it is not a crime for Christians to drink alcohol. In the Gospels, we learn that Jesus' first miracle was turning water into wine during a wedding at Cana in Galilee. So clearly God is not opposed. It is each person's choice whether to drink or not. But the Bible is quite clear in saying we should not be a 'drunkard' (a person who drinks habitually or excessively). Reasonable enough right? Even in today's day and age, I think we can all agree it is best not to be a 'drunkard' and we all should drink responsibly. Regardless, drinking alcohol is each person's choice and is between them and God. It is one of those topics that should not be judged by others.

Now back to the party which was starting to wind down. I was sitting with a group of women, some I had just met for the first time that night, and I of course mentioned to the group that I taught a women's Bible Study and invited them to join.

One woman blurted out, "What are you? One of those Bible thumpers?" Instead of being put-off by her question, I immediately started laughing, and thought it was hilarious since no one had ever called me a 'Bible thumper' before. Everyone else started laughing as well, which clearly softened the woman. As I was still laughing, I quickly replied, "No, not quite."

Another woman who was already coming to the Bible Study chimed in and said, "Oh you should come, it's so great. You'll get so much out of it and it truly has helped me through some really difficult times." With a curious look on her face, the woman looked at me and surprisingly enough, asked me where and what time. I told her we meet at my house, every Tuesday morning at 10:00 am.

    Well, the rest is history. To this day she and I still laugh about that night and I'm now the one calling her the 'Bible thumper'. She has been coming to the Bible Study ever since and she is so thankful for the positive change it has brought to her life which now reflects on her family. She, along with her husband and children are now going to church together and it has made a positive impact in all of their lives.

Chapter 14

WHY DO BAD THINGS HAPPEN TO GOOD PEOPLE?

So why do bad things happen to good people? Ah, yes. The question of all questions. And probably the number one, most asked question by every person in the world—especially after a horrific tragedy. This question alone, should point to the fact that this world is not functioning how it was originally intended to be.

The present evil system is in complete opposition of God. Satan doesn't actually rule the world, but God allows him to be the ruler over the current system of sinful opposition. In other words, Satan is leading the rebellion against God. And believe it or not, God planned it this way. The Bible is clear in telling us that nothing happens by chance, accident or even coincidence. God does what He wants to do, when He wants to do it, in the way He wants to do it, for the purpose He wants to accomplish, and involves any person or persons He chooses to use. God is in complete control. Yet, He still gives us free will.

We are all free to decide how we spend our money, where we drive our cars, who we marry, what career path we should follow and so on. So herein lies the theological paradox. How does God's sovereignty and human free will go together? It's one of the longest running debates of all time. But here's what we can be sure of: God is not controlling, and He does not control us. He does not give us free will then take it away. He offers us blessing and cursing, life and death. He gives us options.

Which leads back to the popular questions. If there really is a God, then why would He allow bad things to happen to good people? Or, if God is sovereign and controls all things, then why would He even create the human race if He already knew we were going to disobey him? Or why would He allow sin and evil to even enter this world? For anyone questioning the existence of God, these are by far the greatest questions of all. Ones that I myself wrestled with even after my relationship with Jesus began.

I once came across the following quote written by an atheist: "Christian theology is incoherent to the point of absurdity. God killing his son so he can forgive our future sin is like me breaking my son's legs so I can forgive my neighbor in case she ever parks her car in my driveway. The whole thing is quite ridiculous." I must be honest, this quote made me second guess and think to myself once again, "Could this atheist be right?"

With this knowledge, my mind formed an image of God where He was looking down upon the human race on earth, from His Heavenly throne, as if He was looking down upon a giant chess match and he was playing both sides of the board. He was in control of both the black and the white chess pieces. This thought was frustrating to me and if this was truly the case, then what was God's point in all this? If He was sovereign and in control of everything, both the good and the evil, then what was the point?

My mind wrestled with this like crazy, until I finally had a little bit of peace after reading the following scripture: Romans 9:20-22 says, "Who are you, a mere human being, to argue with God? Should the thing that was created say to the one who created it, "Why have you made me like this?" When a potter makes jars out of clay, doesn't he have a right to use the same lump of clay to make one jar for decoration and another to throw garbage into?" Reading this scripture did help me arrive at a place of acceptance (yet still somewhat reluctantly), by under-standing that God, as All-Mighty Creator, has every right to do what-ever He wants and answers to no one. But I still wasn't completely satisfied.

It wasn't until my husband Timmy and I met with our friends Donny and Kristi one night when I finally had extreme peace and clarity on the subject. We were discussing this very topic and I told them about the quote from the atheist I had read and how I continued to wrestle with the question of why. Why would a sovereign God knowingly allow both good and evil to exist in this world? That night, Donny, who used to be a Pastor but is now working in the business world, reminded me and highlighted the key component I was missing and the one most people miss—and that is LOVE. A deep-rooted love that our Mighty Creator has for each and every one of us.

Donny continued explaining that the quote from the atheist, breaking his son's legs so he could forgive his neighbor in case she ever parked her car in his driveway, was clearly lacking the deep rooted, unconditional love that God has for us because the atheist did not create his neighbor. In other words, the atheist does not have that same parental, unconditional love toward his neighbor as our Mighty Creator, God, has for us. That is the difference—the BIG difference. I now see clearly what a very poor analogy that was because of the primary missing ingredient—LOVE. God created us and He loves us, more so than our human brains can comprehend or fathom. Just as a father or mother loves their child, what father or mother wouldn't go to excessive lengths in order to save their child?

That is what God did for us. And the evil that God allows in the world does make sense when we understand that we wouldn't have the ability to see or seek God if evil didn't exist. You logically cannot have one without the other. Just like we see the dark of night because we see the sun shining in the day. If all we knew was good, all the time, then not only would we never seek God, but we would also lack depth of character. We would all be shallow, surface dwellers. It's the bad things that happen in our lives that refine us and develop our character. And God cares more about our character than our comfort. It's that old saying, "what doesn't kill you makes you stronger." The bad times always hurt, and are painful, but it is in these times where we are forced to learn, grow and mature.

Without depth of character, we would all be like robots which is exactly the opposite of how God created us. He designed us with a soul and free will and His desire is for us to seek Him and love Him on our own. Without any persuasion or coercion. This is a choice He allows each of us to make. Also, if things were great all the time, how shallow would life and love be? The development of true love requires many levels and layers. Otherwise, we would take it for granted and be unappreciative. God purposefully uses trials in our lives to help us build our spiritual muscles and at the same time, add depth to our characters, enabling us to experience the meaning of love. True love. And as long as we are living here on earth, evil will continue to exist and bad things will continue to happen, because it is the only way we will see our need for God.

Romans 5:3-5 tells us, "We can rejoice, too, when we run into problems and trials, for we know that they help us develop endurance. And endurance develops strength of character, and character strengthens our confident hope of salvation. And this hope will not lead to disappointment. For we know how dearly God loves us, because he has given us the Holy Spirit to fill our hearts with his love." It should give us comfort knowing there is a God who has a good and wise purpose to be served through all our circumstances, including our afflictions.

Think back to a desperate moment in your life. You know what I'm talking about. When something happened that scared you so much that you instinctively prayed and asked for help, perhaps without even knowing who you were praying to. Whether you, or a child or loved one was fighting for their lives, or you were faced with an emergency situation. Whatever it is, our minds will almost instinctively ask for help when faced with sheer desperation.

I remember attending a college party with some girlfriends. We all partook in some drugs that were being passed around. Within twenty minutes I knew something wasn't right. I slowly began to feel funny and panic immediately set in. I was overcome with fear and paranoia. I somehow fumbled my way through the jam-packed party house until I found a remote bathroom located in one of the upstairs bedrooms. I closed the door behind me and locked it. I remember the panic was so overwhelming that I thought I was going to die. I curled up in a corner and in that moment the only thing I could think to do was pray. You know the prayer, the one that goes something like this: "God, if you can help me make it through this night alive, I promise

I will never do this again!" It doesn't matter who you are or what you do or don't believe in, I can guarantee that many of you have found yourself in a similar situation and have done the same thing.

I think in any crisis situation it's almost a normal, sort of knee-jerk reaction for many of us to instinctively pray aloud or within our minds and ask for help. Hoping that someone is listening. We all have a tipping point where we crash (either mentally, physically, emotionally or situationally) and simply need immediate help. In that moment we are all hoping there is something or someone greater than us out there. Someone that will hear our desperate cry and come to our rescue. Well, there is.

All you need to do is ask. Call it a coincidence or whatever you want, but in that moment, my life seemed to be teetering on the brink and after suffering through several hours of fear and panic, I was certainly happy to make it through that night alive. But was that night a life-defining moment for me? Did I truly believe in God after that night? The honest answer is no, but looking back, I can see it was at least a step in the right direction.

I have often looked back on the day I found out my birth mother was murdered. I blamed God and hated him for that. The question of why I was never able to meet her, haunted me for years. It wasn't until I became a Christ follower and was praying about it that I finally had my closure. I remember praying and asking God for an answer because I needed to have peace with it, once and for all.

God finally revealed the answer to me, as if He supernaturally dropped the answer inside my head. I was able to understand that if my birth mother was still alive and I did meet her, I would have never continued on my path in search of God. I was searching for true love and was convinced that my birth mom would have satisfied this. However, it would have been another temporary fix and I would have still come up short because I now understand that no other human can completely satisfy our inner longing and fill that void. Only our Creator can.

And I now see the silver lining, even in that situation. One of my childhood dreams was to have a big family and that dream is now fulfilled with my new extended biological family on both my mother and father's side. I have my wonderful biological father Andy, three half-sisters, a half-brother, many aunts, uncles and cousins who were all hoping and praying I would come back into their lives. And as devastated as they all were when my mom was murdered, it gave them great joy to meet me and welcome me into their lives, especially since I looked exactly like her. And strangely enough, when I first walked into the room to meet my family for the first time, it was shocking because I recognized many of them!

I had known my Grandfather (my birth mother's dad) and my uncle (my birth mother's little brother) from places where I used to work in Newport, RI, and I recognized and personally knew some of my cousins whom I went to the University of Rhode Island with. To think I had known and had relationships with people that I was related to was just crazy. It's mind-blowing to think these people were directly connected to my mom. I was so close, yet so far.

But to this day, I am so thankful for the gift of knowing the circumstances surrounding why I was given up for adoption and to now have a new, extended family. In hopes I would go looking for her sooner than I did, my birth mother wrote me a beautiful letter on my tenth birthday and sent it to the adoption agency where they placed it in my folder. Twenty years later, when I finally went to find her, it was presented to me:

September 12, 1980

>I do not know how to address this letter to you. I want to say, "To My Dearest Daughter," but those words do not seem to be enough.
>
>To say you are dear to me does not come close to expressing my feelings.
>
>Your question of "Why?", perhaps shared with some bitter-ness, cannot simply be answered with my telling you that I have loved you from the moment I first felt your movement within me, and that I will love you forever...
>
>You have questions that need answers, and I want to give you those answers.
>
>You are ten years old today. A very special day in your life. For me, a day that marks so many days of wondering. So

many days of missing you. So many days of hoping you are happy. So many days of loving you.

I pray to God that you are happy and healthy. I pray also that you do not hate me or feel that I deserted you.

I do love you, please believe me.

I truly hope that the day will come when I will finally see you. I never have, you know, for had I, you would now be with me, and not where you were meant to be. But this decision, as to whether or not to see me, is entirely your own. Please don't let what I have just said about wanting to see you, interfere with the feeling you have in your own heart.

For so many years I questioned "Why?" also. And it was only with prayer and time, that I came to understand why… You were chosen, not to be with me, but to be with a family that you could give everything to… yourself.

Had I not loved you so deeply, you would be with me… But being with me was all I could have promised you. It's just that you deserved SO MUCH MORE!

Please believe that I love you.
Your mother, Jeanne

As if both she and God knew the outcome in advance, this letter answered everything. Knowing I would never meet her here on earth, I was provided with my much-needed answers, combined with peace, clarity and closure. Just knowing how much she truly did love me and how much it broke her heart to have made the most difficult, yet selfless, decision of her life. So now I can look forward to seeing her in Heaven. God is always faithful in providing the answers to our questions/prayers when we need them most.

Tragedies happen to us all, they are unavoidable. Some may be worse than others, but one fact remains, we should not allow the tragedy itself to define us, but rather, how we handle or navigate through such tragedies. Sometimes this is easier said than done because when we least expect it, life will present us with a tragedy that will completely blind-side us.

This past year, a very dear friend of mine lost her husband to suicide. This was beyond shocking, heartbreaking and devastating to us all. They were the absolute perfect, loving couple, with a beautiful family. He was a Lieutenant in the Fire Department. He had worked as a first responder for 19 years. Now, how am I supposed to comfort her by telling her that God has a plan through all this? The answer is, I'm not. How can I help her make sense of this or help give her peace? The answer is, I can't. The truth is, first responders, including fire fighters, paramedics, and police officers are more likely to die by suicide than in the line of duty. What they see day after day for years straight is something none of us should see even once in our lifetime. Our minds are not made to erase what we have seen, and for them, what they see compiles over time. And yet they willingly put themselves in harm's way because of their selfless desire to help the people in their communities.

Similar to a war veteran, they are the true heroes, but they too can suffer from PTSD, depression, anxiety and the like. And the hardest part for them is admitting they are feeling depressed or anxious because of the stigma associated with it. They do not want to risk being demoted or even losing their jobs. They don't want to be perceived as weak or looked down upon by their peers so instead they keep it bottled up. This must change! I heard on the news that suicide for first responders is becoming an epidemic and PTSD must be taken seriously. It is a topic that should be openly discussed, proactively addressed and preventative measures must be taken.

As I mentioned previously in my *Spiritual Warfare* chapter; it's through our minds that the enemy sneaks in to attack our thoughts and feed us lies. Here is a beautiful tribute that was written by another friend of ours, his best friend and co-worker at the same Fire Department:

> "PTSD, anxiety and depression are truly ugly. They lied to my friend. They told him that he was worthless. A burden. Unlovable. Undeserving of life. In my eyes, he was simply broken, and I wanted to put him back together. He had one of the biggest hearts I've ever seen crammed into one person. He so often gave of himself, whether it was his smile, his time, his

strength, his knowledge, or just a simple hug. These were his coping mechanisms, because it was making others smile that got him through his struggle day after day. But it was not possible for any of us to fight this battle for him… His life will not be judged by the final page in its story but by the contents of its whole. At times like these, I am reminded how short life really is, and how we are merely passing through. This is a crazy game – LIFE – that we all go through. So, all the people you haven't told you love lately, tell them, and live your days like you truly mean it. Rest easy my brother. I LOVE YOU."

Our friend became a fire-fighter to help save lives, and in the end, it was his own life he couldn't save. I do not look at him as taking his own life, rather, he lost his life to *Spiritual Cancer*. He was unknowingly battling the disease, which led to the enemy feeding him lies. He was tragically manipulated. This was not supposed to be part of the plan and it is times like these that become true wake-up calls. Senselessly losing a beautiful person whom we were so close to, goes to show none of us are immune.

The lies that the enemy feeds are just that. LIES. As if his mind was not able to think rationally about the consequences. Now he has left behind a beautiful wife, three beautiful children and a large, devastated group of family and friends. We must realize that none of us have the power to do this life alone. None of us on our own, have the power to fix ourselves and none of us on our own, have the coping mechanisms to deal with such tragic circumstances.

Stigma's associated with PTSD must be eliminated and it should be widely accepted and perhaps considered normal, for anyone who needs to seek treatment in the form of counseling, antidepressant medications or both. Somehow their minds need to relax enough so that the process of healing and thinking rationally can begin again. Once this healing and re-boot of the mind takes place, then with God's help, they can once again know and believe the truth, instead of the enemies lies, and be fully cured and made new again.

I can only pray that the tragic death of our friend will light the path for others who are suffering with the same symptoms; anxiety, depression, sleeplessness, whatever it is. And I pray that even with our friends passing, his tragic story will help save the lives of others, ensuring that his God-given mission as a first responder will continue on.

I have no words to comfort my friend right now. Nothing seems appropriate. And that's okay. Because I, and everyone close to her, have learned that words aren't necessary. What's most important is the time spent with her, which gives her great comfort knowing her loved ones are close by.

That is also how I would describe a relationship with Jesus. You may not hear His audible voice speaking to you, but knowing He is with you, by your side is the greatest comfort of all. Trusting and knowing you are loved and that He will somehow work things out on your behalf. So I will continue to love on her and be there for her—by her side. And I will continue praying for her and her family. Because I have seen and experienced enough silver-linings myself, to trust and believe that somehow through this tragedy, there will be a silver lining for her and her precious family as well.

The unfortunate part of life is that we all will experience some form of trauma and tragedy. And the question of 'why' may never be answered. But that is when our trust and faith need to kick in. Because for me, even as I look back on the traumatic events I went through with my ex-husband Steve, I have three major things to be thankful for: the birth of my beautiful daughter, finding my husband now and most importantly, finding and experiencing God once and for all. Not only are these the three most important things in my life, but my greatest gifts. It was those gut-wrenching circumstances with Steve that brought me to my knees as I pleaded with God to answer my prayers and help me. God showed up each time I prayed as He clearly used those ugly circumstances to grab my attention. Leave it to God, to take the worst tragedies in our lives and turn them into our greatest blessings.

I remember watching the movie Passion of the Christ, directed by Mel Gibson in 2004. At the time the movie was released, I was nowhere close to believing in God. But even as a non-believer, my eyes welled up with tears during the scenes where the Roman soldiers were brutally beating Jesus (brilliantly played by Jim Caviezel) until He was unrecognizable. Then He was forced to carry

His own cross up the mount where His wrists and feet were then graphically nailed to the wooden cross before it was lifted up and then dropped into the ground where He hung to His death. For those of you who saw it, it was brutal. Of course, this was a movie, but the facts detailing the events are written just as explicitly within the pages of the Bible. It is historical fact and it really did happen just as it was portrayed.

As I watched this scene, I was overwhelmed with sadness. Sad because He was wrongly accused and sad for the brutal beatings and humiliation He had to endure. Knowing He had done nothing wrong and was unjustly condemned and sentenced to such brutality. This is where you see the evil and ugly side of humanity.

I remember blaming Judas, Jesus' own disciple. I believed it was all his fault for betraying Jesus and basically selling his whereabouts (for a small amount of money at that) to the Pharisees so they could send soldiers to arrest him. I always thought, if only Judas didn't betray Him, He wouldn't have had to endure any of it.

What I didn't realize, until I read the Bible myself, is that the crucifixion and death of Jesus was all part of God's master plan from the very beginning of time. Because of the immense love He has for all humanity, Jesus willingly came to earth for that very moment, in order to save the human race from sin. So it's interesting to see that Judas' betrayal of Jesus was predestined and ordained by God. God basically used Judas as a pawn in order to fulfill His purpose—to come to earth and willing die and sacrifice Himself for the very sins that I, and all of us deal with. And still to this day, God will purposefully use evil (or what we perceive as evil) in our lives, for His good in order to fulfill His purpose and plan for each of us.

So when we ask the question again, "Why do bad things happen to good people?" We must remember this: there never was nor has there been a better or greater person known in history, than Jesus. So if Jesus Himself, God in human form, perfect in every way, who never sinned—had to endure a life where he was persecuted, hated, mocked and scorned by people during his life and then brutally beaten and hung on a cross to His death (basically murdered), then we too will face trials and tragedy as well. Jesus knew exactly what He was doing and what the end game would be.

We were never meant to do life alone. This was Gods master plan to reconcile our relationship with Him. So Jesus' selfless sacrifice for us was a perfect example for us all to see—that the greatest of blessings comes through the worst of trials. There is nothing now in this life that we can go through that Jesus Himself did not have to endure.

Jesus came to earth as the original first responder. His sole mission was to save our lives at the cost of his own.

He is the greatest of all leaders and the epitome of leading by example. Each trial in life will either draw you one step closer to Him or one step further away and because He has given us free will, the choice will always be our own.

Chapter 15

FACT IS STRANGER THAN FICTION

For those of you who may still be on the fence, questioning if God is real or not. This story just might help put you over the edge.

Timmy and I were married in December 2011 and this was a dream-come-true for ParisElla, who was 4 years old at the time. I first met Timmy when I was pregnant with her and she had known him ever since she could remember. She was even a baby model for horse-themed onesies in our JPC Equestrian catalog before she could even crawl. She grew up knowing Timmy. And even though her momma may not have loved, or even liked him back then, she sure did.

I will never forget the day we announced to her we were getting married—she was clearly elated. She referred to our wedding as 'her wedding', which as a mother, just warmed my heart. During the ceremony, Timmy brought her up in front of our guests, got down on one knee and made a promise to her that he would love and protect her as if she was his own, and then he placed a sweet little ring on her left ring finger as well. There wasn't a dry eye in the room.

God provided me my Indian Prince Charming and my fairy-tale ending. But that didn't mean everything was peachy and perfect from thereon in. Life still had and continues to have its ups and down. Even through the bad times though, my life has changed for the better. The trust and faith I have now in Jesus gives me such strength and confidence with any situation that comes my way. Even the toughest of situations. Allow me to explain.

When I divorced Steve, ParisElla's biological father, in 2006, he agreed to supervised visitation. It was the beginning of 2012, just a few months after Timmy and I had been married, when I received papers from an attorney stating Steve wanting to now fight for 50/50 custody of ParisElla. Panic immediately set in. Ironically, I had just met a female attorney at a friend's house, who practiced family law, so I quickly reached out to her to represent me with this. Not too long after, she told me a mediation date had been set where Steve and I would hopefully come to an agreement without having to go court. I was strong in my convictions and was certain I did not want anything to change since this was a man whom I was not able to trust, especially with my daughter.

One week prior, I was teaching a Bible Study Wednesday morning—yup, that's right, the very same Bible Study I didn't want to attend initially, the one where I felt completely out of place, was the same one I had now been asked to teach. God's plans sure aren't our plans! Well, it was that day when I told the entire room, filled with prayer warrior women, what I was about to embark on. I told them the entire story and asked them to pray for me and ParisElla.

The following Tuesday was the mediation. I met with my attorney at our local courthouse. She quickly briefed me on what was about to happen. She and I sat in a room while Steve and his attorney sat in another. The mediator was to go back and forth between rooms until we hopefully, came to a mutual agreement.

An hour or so went by before the mediator came into our room. He spoke with Steve and his attorney first. He sat down and basically told me there was no sense arguing or fighting this case. He explained it was clear to him that Steve, as the biological father, was going to get shared custody of ParisElla. I immediately spoke up and said I would not agree to this and proceeded to tell him the reasons why I wanted to keep with the original agreement of supervised visitation.

He looked at me and said matter-of-factly, "Well, that may have been the case, but Steve has never been caught or accused of anything, nor does he have a record." I replied, "Just because he hasn't been caught or arrested, doesn't mean he isn't capable." Getting obviously irritated with me he took off his glasses, leaned forward and said, "Look Mrs. Sharma, I just retired as a judge and sat on the bench of family court for the last twenty-some-odd years. So I can tell you right now that you do not have a leg to stand on and Steve, with no prior record, will absolutely be awarded 50/50 custody of his daughter. I have certainly seen it all over the years, and even if this was to go to trial, which I hope for your sake it doesn't, you will lose." He continued, "So the best thing for you to do right now is just figure out a custody schedule that will work best for you both."

I took a deep breath and as calmly as I could, I said, "With all due respect sir, I am not going to give this up without a fight because I know what he is capable of, especially when he drinks." I continued to tell the mediator different examples of the things he admitted to me that night. He abruptly cut me off and said something so shocking I will never forget, "Well, he didn't admit to having intercourse with her, did he?" I exclaimed, "No!" He continued, "Well what do you care, as long as he's not having intercourse with her?"

Are you freaking kidding me! Did he really just say what I think he said? My eyes opened wide with shock as I stared in horror at this sick, twisted and perverted man. I then looked angrily over at my attorney, as she stared back at me like a deer in headlights, waiting for her to say something, which she never did. My eyes welled up with tears and I immediately stood up, ran out of the room and slammed the door behind me, thinking to myself, "Is this really our terrific judicial system? Seriously?"

Once again, I sought out the nearest restroom where I could be alone. I again fell to the floor sobbing. But this time was thankfully different. Although this circumstance was far worse than my last desperate bathroom moment, I at least knew Who I could turn to and Who had my back.

Although still scared for my daughter's sake, I knew deep down that with everything else God had control over, He surely had control over this situation as well. I left the courthouse and immediately called Timmy on my way home and explained what had just happened. He too was in shock. Needless to say, we fired that attorney and immediately found another.

The next day was Wednesday and I went to my Bible Study. As soon as I walked in, everyone asked how the mediation went. I barely made it to the center of the room when I fell to my knees and started sobbing. I told them what had happened, and everyone was horrified. Clearly no one expected a twist like this to my story. I instinctively did the only thing I could think to do. With my hands wide open, palms up and pressed together side-by-side, I raised them above my head as I spoke these words aloud through my tears, "I surrender my daughter to you Lord, she belongs to you, she is yours, not mine. You have allowed me to be her mother but now I surrender her into your Mighty Hands. I know you have ultimate control of this situation and I trust you will only allow what is best for her."

All the women huddled around me; they hugged me, cried with me and prayed with me. A mother's strongest desire is to protect her child. And here I was in a situation once again where I had zero control over the outcome.

One woman quickly grabbed her Bible, flipped to the following scripture, and started reading aloud, Joshua 1:9, "Be strong and courageous. Do not be afraid; do not be discouraged, for the LORD your God will be with you wherever you go." Another woman followed her by reading Psalm 118:6-7, "The LORD is with me, so I will have no fear. What can mere people do to me? Yes, the LORD is with me; he will help me. I look in triumph on my enemies. The LORD is with me; I will not be afraid." A third woman spoke up and read; Philippians 4:6-7, "Don't worry about anything; instead pray about everything. Tell God what you need and thank him for all he has done. Then you will experience God's peace which exceeds anything we can understand."

There I was, in the grips of fear and desperation, yet hearing these scriptures was the exact medicine my soul needed and a perfect reminder of the battle that is raging around us. And the assurance that our Mighty God is in complete control. I was immediately overcome with the supernatural peace and comfort that only He can provide. And such a perfect example of standing on that foundation of truth within scripture and winning that battle of 'spiritual warfare' that I mentioned in the previous chapter. To this day, these are three of my favorite scriptures that I have since memorized and will say to myself whenever I am overcome with fear or doubt. I am not letting that enemy win!

A few days later, as I was cleaning the kitchen and having my daily prayer dialogue with God, it came to me. I ran into Timmy's office and said, "Babe, if you were able, would you want to legally adopt ParisElla?" Without hesitation he replied, "Of course I would." I immediately picked up my phone and called our new attorney and asked him what the process would be for Timmy to legally adopt ParisElla. He explained it rarely happens because Steve would need to agree to sign over all parental rights, which he said was basically unheard of. He said there are men sitting in jail, with no hope of ever getting out, who still wouldn't sign over their child's parental rights to anyone else.

I said to him, "I understand this is far-fetched, but would you please do me a favor and just call Steve and ask him if there is any way he would consider allowing Timmy to legally adopt her?" He laughed and said, "I don't think we'll get very far if I do that." He continued, "I can almost guarantee, the way he is fighting for shared custody, he will never agree to it." I said, "Please do me this favor and just ask him." He reluctantly agreed and said he would call him first thing in the morning as he forewarned me once again to not get my hopes up.

That night, I just prayed, and prayed and prayed. The next afternoon I received a call from our attorney. He said, "Hi Laurie, I spoke with Steve." I nervously replied, "And?" "Well, he didn't say no," he said. With a huge smile on my face, I asked him again just to make sure I heard him correctly, "What did you say?" He said again, "He didn't say no." I was so incredibly shocked and surprised yet filled with such joy. At that moment I knew with all my heart that God was once again at work behind the scenes.

Our attorney then went into details about their conversation. "Evidently Steve is quite concerned with the $10,000 he owes you for back-pay from child support. He wants to know if he would still owe you that money." I quickly replied, "Of course not!" He continued, "He also wants to know if he would be liable for any other child support going forward." Again, I replied, "Absolutely not! He wouldn't have to pay anything ever again. No school tuition, health insurance, nothing." Again, he continued, "He also wants to know if you will still allow him to speak with ParisElla and sometimes see her." Again,

I agreed, knowing it would be on my terms. He then said, "Okay, I will have another conversation with him tomorrow and let him know."

The following afternoon, our attorney called and said he spoke with Steve and he seemed quite agreeable to everything and that he just wanted to have a conversation with me before he made his final decision. I agreed to speak with him. The next day, Steve called, and we spoke on the phone. It was a surprisingly amicable conversation. We went over the financial issues again and I assured him he would no longer be obligated to financially support ParisElla. He then expressed some concerns regarding Timmy adopting her because he still wanted to call her and see her. I assured him that this would be fine and reminded him that I too was adopted, so I would never interfere and would allow her to make her own decisions as she grows older.

I had seen and heard of way too many children who have been emotionally destroyed while they were caught in the middle of two separated or divorced parents that are ugly toward each other. I truly believe a child should not hear one parent speak badly about another. No matter how bad the situation is. And I was not going to be one of those parents. I knew I would always allow ParisElla to form her own opinion and make her own decisions as she gets older; so, I agreed, under our current limitations, that we would be willing to do that. By the end of the conversation I could tell Steve felt comfortable with the decision and was ready to move forward.

Our attorney called the next day and asked about the conversation. I told him it went well and based on what he and I discussed, it seemed Steve was onboard. He could not believe it. He was very happy and hopeful for us but still could not believe it.

With that said, he did prepare us for another potential hurdle and said, "Listen, I don't want to burst your bubble but Steve could be agreeing to it now, but as soon as I send him the paperwork and he reads the documentation, chances are he will change his mind because the verbiage is really scary". He continued, "It specifically states that he is willingly signing over ALL parental rights to any and all decisions and so on, on behalf of his biological daughter, ParisElla." Again, he repeated, "He might be agreeing to it now, but just be prepared, that when he reads the legal document, he may back off. Especially since he will not only have to sign it, but he will also need to have it notarized in order for it to legally hold up in a court of law."

Once again, worry tried to wiggle its way inside my head as I pondered the 'what-if's'. What if after all this, Steve does change his mind? What if he decides not to sign over parental rights to Timmy? I was hit hard again by a wave of fear and panic. But instead of festering on those negative thoughts, I quickly recognized it as the enemy trying to feed me lies and remembered the scripture; Psalm 118:6-7, that instantly eased my mind by reminding me, "The LORD is with me, so I will have no fear. What can mere people do to me? Yes, the LORD is with me; he will help me. I look in triumph on my enemies. The LORD is with me; I will not be afraid." Another perfect example of how we can put our faith into action and use God's word of truth to help us fight our spiritual battles. I again experienced His supernatural peace and didn't give it another thought.

Our attorney sent Steve the paperwork and as days went by, we heard nothing. Our attorney then called him to follow-up and Steve told him he would be sending the signed documents soon. More days went by, which turned into weeks...

Every day I continued to pray, begging God to allow this to happen, when finally, the celebratory call came from our attorney. "I just received Steve's signed and notarized paperwork!" He was so happy for us and said he would schedule a court date as soon as possible for ParisElla's legal adoption. We were moved to tears with this joyous news and once again, in awe of our amazing God!

We had decided previously not to say anything to ParisElla, who was only 5 years old at the time, because we didn't want to get her hopes up. She was certainly old enough to understand and know what was going on. As it was, when Timmy and I were married, she was really upset that her last name couldn't be Sharma too. From a 5-year-old's point of view, she assumed it was an easy enough thing to change, so I had already explained to her why it wasn't so easy.

So needless to say, we were beyond excited to share this great news with her. The three of us sat together in our living room that night as Timmy and I prepared ourselves to have our very first grown-up conversation with her. I said, "ParisElla, we have some very exciting news to share with you." She immediately exclaimed, "What mommy, what?" As she excitedly began kicking her little legs I said, "How would you like your last name to be Sharma?" She looked at Timmy (who she calls Papi), covered her little hands to her mouth and said, "Really mommy?" She giggled and said, "You know I would love that! But how? I thought you said I'm not able to have that last name?" I said, "Well honey, Papi and I have been praying a lot for this day and God has just made it possible for Papi to adopt you and legally be your daddy.

Timmy then said to her, "So ParisElla, if it's okay with you, you have the choice now to officially be my daughter which means you will also have the last name of Sharma, so, would you accept me as your Daddy?" Tiny little happy tears ran down her cheeks and she looked at us both and said, "Oh that would make me so very happy Papi!" She leaned into us both for a big group hug. She then said, "Mommy, now I'll be like you, just like you were adopted, Papi is also adopting me. Look at how God answered all of our prayers!" She exclaimed, "He is the best!" We all cried happy tears and thanked God for showing us once again how real, how in control, how powerful, and how loving He truly is.

The court date was scheduled just one week after Steve signed the papers. The three of us got ready and appeared in the court room. Excitement was written all over our faces. The judge said a few things to our attorney, and before we knew it, it was official. The judge asked ParisElla if she was excited about her new daddy and she exclaimed "I sure am!" He then invited her up to his bench, he got up from his seat and allowed her to sit there and said, "Okay, now in order to make this official, you need to hit this hammer right on this wooden square." And she did just as he said. What a glorious day.

Our attorney knelt down and sweetly congratulated ParisElla and gave her a big hug. As he got back up, he looked at Timmy and I and quietly said, "There is just one more thing. We're not quite out of the woods yet." "Ugh, what now?" I said. As we were walking out, our attorney explained that even though we finalized the adoption today, Steve will still have one year to withdraw his decision. And if he changes his mind and decides for any reason, he doesn't want the adoption to happen, then we will be back to square one.

As much as my brain (the enemy) wanted me to be upset by this news, I already knew in my heart what the outcome would be. All I had to do was stay focused on God and continue to trust in His faithfulness which He had shown me vividly time and time again over the past few years. And that, need I say, was enough to keep me strong and positive. Deep down, I knew if God had taken us this far, He would surely see us through to the end.

Throughout the year, Steve would call ParisElla on the phone and speak with her. We also arranged a couple times for him to see her that year. The anniversary date of the adoption date was now close at hand and I counted down the days leading up to it. Hoping and praying all along that the call from Steve changing his mind would never come. The anniversary day arrived and the three of us went out to dinner to officially celebrate.

The very next day, my phone rang, and it was Steve. He asked to see ParisElla that weekend and I explained to him we already had plans. He immediately got angry and threatened to take me back to court and fight for shared custody again. Literally one year and one day later. Once again, a powerful moment illuminating the supreme control and true reality of our sovereign God.

I calmly said to him, "Steve, you can't fight this in court anymore. You have signed over all parental rights. Timmy is now her legal father." He angrily snapped back, "What are you talking about?" "What do you mean what am I talking about?" I said, "Don't you remember? You signed a paper…" He immediately interrupted me before I could finish my sentence and said, "I didn't sign anything!" I replied, "But you did, and not only did you sign it, but you had it notarized." "Well there hasn't been a court date yet," he said. "Yes, there has," I said. "When?" he asked. I told him our court date was one year ago. He said, "Well I don't know how that happened since I wasn't told about it." I then said, "Please do me a favor and call my attorney and speak with him about it." He gruffly replied, "I will."

Our attorney called me within minutes and said, "Steve just called me. Can you believe he has absolutely no recollection of signing those papers?" I said, "Yeah, I know, he told me the same thing."

Coincidence? Again, I'll let you decide. But to us, it was just another crystal-clear example of how God is mightily at work behind the scenes in our lives. The timing was far too perfect to brush it off as merely a coincidence. This clearly was another undeniable answer to prayer.

Please understand, I have not written any of this to try convert you or brainwash you or even try to convince you of anything because quite frankly, I don't have the power. My only desire is to be like that farmer I mentioned previously, and plant seeds in your mind by sharing how God miraculously transformed my life and my family's life, in hopes that you too will take a step back and think for a moment about your life and/or your family's life. I simply want to encourage you to do the same thing I did—ask for His help and see for yourself. You have nothing to lose and everything to gain.

I look at it this way, I was given an amazing free gift that dramatically changed my life in ways I never dreamed possible. So how selfish would I be to not share this amazing gift with you or anyone else. And like I said it's free! Other than free shipping for Amazon Prime members, how often are we offered anything for free? Especially something like this. There truly is nothing greater!

As I said before, it would be awful if I had the cure for physical cancer and didn't share it. But I do know the cure for this *Spiritual Cancer*, and it is now my life's mission and purpose to share it with as many people as possible.

Chapter 16

CHOOSING LIFE or DEATH

Here's the cold, hard truth: At any given moment, you could die. We all will die. We all have an expiration date and every day we wake up; we are one day closer to our demise. Every cemetery testifies that our days on this earth are numbered. It could be today, tomorrow, or even 50 years from now—but we all will face the inevitable at some point. This may sound morbid, but it is the truth and it is a reality.

A devastating tragedy, like the loss of a loved one, could happen to any of us at any moment. It's only when we are hit hard with something like this that we are reminded of what truly is important, what really matters and how short life is. Only in sickness, disease, or even an injury or accident do we fully understand how fragile life is.

But the sad news is, we are all living for the moment and not understanding that our time here on earth is limited. The thought of what might happen to us when we die is probably not at the forefront of our thoughts. But when it is upon us, death instills fear because of the unknown. But what if there really is a God? What if there really is such thing as heaven or hell? What if I wasn't a good enough person while I was here on earth? What if I did something bad and God doesn't like me? These thoughts may cross our minds at a funeral or in hearing about the death of someone, or we may have a close call with death ourselves. But then, as time goes on, these thoughts of death become a distant memory. But they should be a daily reality because we all are on borrowed time.

People who are in the most danger spiritually are the ones whose pride gets in the way. They cannot accept that they are imperfect or make mistakes (sinners) and they are the ones who don't see their need for God. Life may appear great to them — they may be successful and even looked up to by others; they may even be honest, moral, and generous to others. But none of that is enough.

One of the hardest truths for any of us to accept is that there is absolutely nothing we can do on our own to earn our acceptance with God and gain access into heaven. We all think that if we do good deeds, if we are generous, or honest, or compassionate, then that's good enough. But the truth is, nothing we can do will ever be enough. We all are infected with this *Spiritual Cancer*. God is holy and His standard is perfection and we are all imperfect human beings. Just the thought of us thinking we are good enough only proves how imperfect (prideful) we are — and pride is a sin. Do you now see how sneaky sin is and how fallen humanity is? It's only when we see ourselves as God sees us — with our imperfections — that we realize our need for a savior.

But here is the really good news. Despite our imperfections (sin), God still loves us. So much so that he sent His son Jesus, to die on the cross for us. All we need to do is believe and receive. Believe Christ died for us, and by faith, receive Him into our lives. It's that simple and the greatest gift of all.

This is summed up perfectly in Ephesians 2:8-10, "God saved you by his grace when you believed. And you can't take credit for this; it is a gift from God. Salvation is not a reward for the good things we have done, so none of us can boast about it. For we are God's masterpiece." There is nothing we can do to work for or earn this right. He freely offers it to each and every one of us in the form of grace. Grace is one of the most beautiful and wonderful words of all time. Grace is the free and unmerited favor of God. Not one of us can earn or win our salvation with our 'good deeds', but that's okay, because Jesus has already earned and won it for the entire human race! And it's never too late to accept and receive this free gift.

When Jesus was crucified, there were two other criminals who were also crucified alongside Him. One of the greatest and most immediate redemptive stories occurred while Jesus and these two criminals were hanging on the crosses side-by-side, during their crucifixions.

Luke 23:39-43, "One of the criminals hanging beside him scoffed, "So you're the Messiah, are you? Prove it by saving yourself—and us, too, while you're at it!" But the other criminal protested, "Don't you fear God even when you have been sentenced to die? We deserve to die for our crimes, but this man hasn't done anything wrong." Then he said, "Jesus, remember me when you come into your Kingdom." And Jesus replied, "I assure you, today you will be with me in paradise."

Notice how one of the criminals mocked Jesus while they were dying on the cross and the other criminal called out to Jesus, recognized Him for who He was and asked Jesus to remember Him. Jesus recognized this criminal's repentant heart and in an instant, with one quick sentence, forgave the man's sins by stating he would be with Jesus today in paradise. Assuring him his soul would be with Him in heaven.

Note some things about the criminal's beliefs.

- He acknowledged the existence of God.
- He believed in a standard of right and wrong.
- He confessed that he and his buddy had committed a crime.
- He admitted that he and his buddy were being punished justly.

The other criminal however, even throughout his agonizing torture on the cross, literally joined his torturers in insulting the Savior of the world. It seems he did this because he wanted everyone to think he was just like them; joined to the world with no love or reverence for God. So even though this man witnessed the salvation of his friend by the Savior right next to him, it was his personal pride that kept him from submitting to the only One who could save him. So here goes to show, no matter how minor or extreme our mistakes (sins) may be, it is never too late to come clean and ask Jesus to forgive us.

So let me ask you this. Is your pride still telling you that God doesn't exist, or that you don't need Him? Do you really think you've got this whole 'life thing' under control? Are you so hardened to your surroundings that you can't see the tangible proof of His splendor and magnificence daily? Just go back to my chapter on science. My plea is this; please do not be like the criminal on the cross who scoffed at Jesus and was blinded by his pride, even as he faced death. Wouldn't it be a better option to be like the other criminal who saw Jesus for who He really was and then when facing death, he was assured that he would be joining Jesus in eternal Heavenly paradise?

There's a great saying by Lecrae, a Grammy Award winning rapper who is also Christian: "If I'm wrong about God then I wasted my life. If you're wrong about God, then you wasted your eternity."

God's love provides a plan of redemption and salvation for a lost and sinful world. Imagine a judge sitting in a courtroom with several perpetrators on trial for committing heinous crimes. The perpetrators robbed countless banks and murdered innocent people in their path, one being your friend or family member. What if the judge overruled the attorneys, witnesses, and jury, and made his own decision to let the perpetrators go free? No sentencing, no penalty, no punishment whatsoever. All judges have the right to do this, by the way. Would you consider this judge to be a good judge? A fair and just judge? Especially after one of the people they shot and killed was your loved one? The answer is, of course not! Well, God is no different.

This leads to the popular question, "If God is so loving then why would He allow anyone to go to hell?" Do you honestly think God should allow people like Hitler or Stalin into heaven and turn a blind eye to their heinous crimes when they never believed in or accepted God while they were alive? Of course not. Anyone who believes in God and is a true Christ follower wouldn't be capable of performing such horrific acts. Otherwise, we would have seen the Apostle Paul continuing to persecute and kill Christians even after his conversion. Every new believer is given the gift of the Holy Spirit that dwells within them and immediately goes to work in transforming their hearts and minds.

Although God is all loving, He is also the judge of all and the judge who sits on His heavenly throne and is fair and just. Sins such as murder and rape are obviously an offense to our holy and pure God, but so are the minor and hidden sins such as, anger, jealousy, pride and worry. God cannot simply ignore sin (no matter how great or small) and pretend it doesn't exist, because to do so would be unjust. If someone hates or disbelieves in God and chooses to do evil, whether consciously or subconsciously, God cannot overlook this rebellion. The Bible is very clear in Acts 17:31, "He has set a day when he will judge the world with justice."

If you think logically about it, there are always consequences for our actions. Perhaps we can outsmart other people and never get caught for our wrongdoings here on earth. But God knows and sees all. Nothing any of us do can escape God. So when we die, and we do stand face-to-face with our mighty Creator, we will no longer have a second chance and we will no longer be second guessing what is written in the Bible. Romans 14: 10-12 says it all, "You, then, why do you judge your brother or sister? Or why do you treat them with contempt? For we will all stand before God's judgment seat. It is written: "'As surely as I live, says the Lord, 'every knee will bow before me; every tongue will confess to God.' "So then, each of us will give an account of ourselves to God."

You may have wondered by now, why I have written and quoted so many scriptures from the Bible. The answer is simple. Because the Bible points to TRUTH. As it is written in John 8:31-32, Jesus said to the people who believed in him, "You are truly my disciples if you remain faithful to my teachings. And you will know the truth, and the truth will set you free." It is the exact foundation, I spoke about in the beginning, from which all truth is established. I'm sure some will disagree and that's okay. For hundreds of years, many people have disagreed and have tried to prove that the Bible is false, and they continuously fall short. There are no contradictions in it whatsoever, and it is filled with real history of real people, who lived, said, and did the things it says they did.

In the late 1970's, Lee Strobel, a journalist and atheist, was married to a woman who converted to Christianity. Mr. Strobel was not happy—to the point he was either going to divorce her or find cold hard facts to prove she had been brainwashed and suckered into some cult. Using his investigative and journalism background, his mission began. Something he assumed he would solve in a weekend, ended up taking him on a two-year journey. The more questions he asked, the more answers he found. He found true evidence that was not only compelling but surprising. By the end of his research, he concluded that it would take more faith to maintain his atheism than to become a Christian. He then documented his journey within the pages of his best-seller *The Case for Christ*.

As Lee Strobel himself found out, the Bible is not a book of fables, mythology or fictitious characters. These were real life people who walked the same earth we inhabit today. He concluded that anyone who tries to make false claims about the Bible does so out of ignorance. He could only say this because he was one of those people. He believed, as did I and most of us do, that the Bible was just an old, ancient, outdated book filled with fables, without ever opening the pages and seeing for himself. He admitted to not only being judgmental, but also ignorant.

People may pick and choose certain scriptures from the Bible and form their own opinions, but two major facts will always remain: the prophecies foretold in the scriptures (except Revelation, which describes the future) have already come to pass and everything the prophets wrote about and predicted in the Old Testament have already happened and have come true.

We've all heard of the heroic acts of Mahatma Gandhi who led a peace treaty against the English wars in India. His inspiration grew out of great respect for Jesus and the extent to which he drew inspiration from Him is revealed in his following statements: "What does Jesus mean to me? To me, he was one of the greatest teachers humanity has ever had."[16] "Jesus lived and died in vain if He did not teach us to regulate the whole of life by the eternal law of love."[17] "Jesus, a man who was completely innocent, offered himself as a sacrifice for the good of others, including his enemies, and became the ransom of the world. It was a perfect act."[18] "Jesus was the most active resister known perhaps to history.

His was non-violence par excellence."[19] "Jesus expressed as no other could, the spirit and will of God. It is in this sense that I see him and recognize him as the Son of God. And because the life of Jesus has the significance and the transcendence to which I have alluded, I believe that he belongs not solely to Christianity but to the entire world, to all races and people. It matters little under what flag, name or doctrine they may work, profess a faith or worship a God inherited from their ancestors."[20]

Gandhi affirms that Jesus is the Son of God and belongs not solely to a religion, but He is for the entire world. Gandhi's great respect for Jesus, however, came only after he went to England and South Africa. In his younger years he had a strong aversion to Christianity. In his autobiography he writes, "That whereas I had learnt from my parents who had many Jain and Moslem friends, to respect religions other than my own, Christianity at that time was an exception.

In those days Christian missionaries used to stand in a corner near the high school and hold forth, pouring abuse on Hindus and their Gods. I could not endure this. I must have stood there only once but that was enough to dissuade me from repeating the experiment. About the same time, I heard of a well-known Hindu having been converted to Christianity. It was the talk of the town that when he was baptized, he had to eat beef, drink liquor and change his clothes and thenceforth go about in English costume including a hat. I also heard that the new convert had begun abusing the religion of his ancestors, their customs and their country. All these things created in me a dislike for Christianity."'[21]

It was in London, toward the end of his second year there, that he was first introduced, through Theosophy, to the Gita, Buddhism and Christianity. Soon thereafter he met a devout Christian, in a vegetarian boarding house, who spoke to him about Christianity. Gandhi confessed his aversion to it since his school days. The Christian replied "I am a vegetarian. I do not eat meat and I do not drink." Many Christians eat meat and drink; but neither meat eating nor drinking defines you as a Christian. Do please read the Bible."[22]

Gandhi agreed and began reading the Bible. Jesus' Sermon on the Mount in the New Testament went straight to his heart. [23] Which inevitably lead to one of Gandhi's most famous quotes: "I like your Christ, I do not like your Christians. Your Christians are so unlike your Christ."

And such is the ongoing plight of humanity. None of us will ever be able to live up to Jesus' standard and live a perfect and holy life. Christian or not, we will all continue to make mistakes because of the *Spiritual Cancer* we are born with.

But (and this is a big but) if you do call yourself a Christian, you must be prepared to walk-the-walk, if you're going to talk-the-talk. There are some people who talk-the-talk by openly praising God, speaking outwardly about their faith, talking about how they go to church, volunteer, donate money and so on. These same people then turn around and do shady business deals, lie to others, lash out, get angry, judge others, continuously talk poorly about others, never apologize and the list goes on. They act anything but Christ-like and we all may know people like this. These are the ones Gandhi was referring to and it saddens me to say that these are the Christians that give Christianity a bad name. And I too am guilty as charged!

Here, we see where Jesus, once again, sets the record straight as He calls people out for these exact wrongdoings. He addresses the crowd in Matthew 15:8-14, "These people honor me with their lips, but their hearts are far from me. Their worship is a farce, for they teach man-made ideas as commands from God.'" Then Jesus called to the crowd to come and hear. "Listen," he said, "and try to understand. It's not what goes into your mouth that defiles you; you are defiled by the words that come out of your mouth." Then the disciples came to him and asked, "Do you realize you offended the Pharisees by what you just said?" Jesus replied, "Every plant not planted by my heavenly Father will be uprooted, so ignore them. They are blind guides leading the blind, and if one blind person guides another, they will both fall into a ditch."

He then goes on to say in Matthew 15:18-20, "But the words you speak come from the heart—that's what defiles you. For from the heart come evil thoughts, murder, adultery, all sexual immorality, theft, lying, and slander. These are what defile you."

You will know and recognize a true Christian by not only their words, but also their actions. It's a heart thing, not a head thing. Once a person accepts Jesus into their lives, their hearts will undergo a purification and cleansing transformation by the power of the Holy Spirit.

I am blown away; not only by how much my life has changed, but how much I have changed as a person since becoming born-again. I can honestly, yet not so proudly admit that I would be outwardly rude, crude, every other word I spoke was a swear word, I'd argue with people, manipulate people and lie. Inwardly, I would hold grudges, be prideful, paranoid, controlling, jealous, stressed out, make selfish choices, you name it. And despite all this, I thought I was normal. I was 37 years old and never felt I needed to change. I believed my thoughts and actions were normal and acceptable. I had no reason to think otherwise. I acted and thought the same way many people do, so I never had any desire or reason to change. Or so I thought. I guess it's that saying, 'you don't know what you don't know.'

Imagine if you were born on a boat and you remained at sea with your parents for your entire life. All you saw while you were growing up was the ocean. Then as an adult, you were hit by a major storm and your boat ran ashore. As you step off the boat, you see sand for the first time, trees for the first time, you see the vibrant colors of flowers as you take in their aromatic smell and the smell of fresh cut grass. You now experience new and different foods, new people, new places and it's all very exciting. Your life before was fine and normal because you didn't know anything else. You never even knew you were missing anything. But now, you've been introduced to entirely new aspects of life. Your life is still the same, just better, more exciting and far more beautiful.

And that is a new life with God. Your life is still your life, just a new and improved version. Many will go through life without even realizing they are missing something—something better that is out there. I never realized it. How can you fix something when you don't even realize it's broken? The simple answer is, you can't.

Or maybe you do feel like something is missing, you just don't know what it is. It's only now, since my life has changed so dramatically for the better, that I can look back and see how broken my life used to be—it has done a complete 180. This change wasn't something I consciously tried to do using my own willpower and self-control. None of it was my doing and it certainly wasn't instant and didn't happen overnight. It is the power of the Holy Spirit that has been working in my life and transforming my heart throughout the past 12 years—to the point I now think differently, speak differently, act differently and see life differently. And this transformation will continue until the day I die; molding and sculpting me into a better version of myself—more like Christ. My desire is for people to see less of me and more of Him.

The best way to describe this change and the visible evidence is found in a passage I mentioned earlier about the *Fruit of the Spirit* in Galatians 5:22-23, "But the fruit of the Spirit is love, joy, peace patience, kindness, goodness, faithfulness, gentleness and self-control." I recently read a powerful analogy from an unknown author:

> You are holding a cup of coffee when someone comes along and bumps into you, making you spill your coffee everywhere.
> Why did you spill the coffee?
> "Well because someone bumped into me, of course!"
> Wrong answer.
> You spilled the coffee because, coffee was in the cup.
> If tea had been in it, you would have spilled tea.
> Whatever is inside the cup is what will come out.
> Therefore, when life comes along and shakes you (which will happen), whatever is inside of you will come out. It's easy to fake it until you get rattled.
> So we have to ask ourselves... what's in my cup?
> When life gets tough, what spills over?
> Joy, gratefulness, peace and humility?
> Or anger, bitterness, harsh words and actions?
> You choose!

The choice is ours. If Jesus Himself came to serve and not be served, then who are we? Are we better than Jesus? Should others bow down to us? Should we look down on, think less of or disrespect others? We all know the well-known Bible verse called The Golden Rule: Matthew 7:12, "Do to others whatever you would like them to do to you."

Jesus' weapon was love and ours should be as well. He came to give sight to the blind, heal the sick, love the unlovable. He put the self-righteous in their place. He lived a life of ultimate humility and then willingly died and sacrificed Himself for our sins, not because He was sinful, but because of the extreme love He has for us. We must understand and accept that none of us are any better, greater or more important than anyone else. We are all created equal and we should act and treat others this way.

Maya Angelou wrote her own version of a famous poem entitled "I am a Christian" which sums it up perfectly:

"When I say… "I am a Christian," I'm not shouting, "I'm clean living." I'm whispering, "I was lost, but now I'm found and forgiven."

When I say… "I am a Christian," I don't speak of this with pride. I'm confessing that I stumble and need Christ to be my guide.

When I say… "I am a Christian," I'm not trying to be strong. I'm professing that I'm weak and need His strength to carry on.

When I say… "I am a Christian," I'm not bragging of success. I'm admitting I have failed and need God to clean my mess.

When I say… "I am a Christian," I'm not claiming to be perfect. My flaws are far too visible, but God believes I am worth it.

When I say… "I am a Christian," I still feel the sting of pain. I have my share of heartaches, so I call upon His name.

When I say… "I am a Christian," I'm not holier than thou. I'm just a simple sinner who received God's good grace, somehow.

Please think about everything I've written thus far and process it. Not long ago, I was exactly where you are. With my doubts, my disbelief, grinding day in and day out and struggling with life in general. I was probably farther from God than most. So rest assured, I have been in your shoes. It's hard to believe in something or someone you cannot see. I get it. But let me just say, if He made a believer out of me, He can make a believer out of you. I'm no different than you. Just the couple of times I prayed; He was right there to answer them so vividly that there was no denying how real He is. And I encourage you to do the same.

He has made my life greater than I ever imagined possible, and for this, I will be eternally grateful. Knowing that Jesus came to sacrifice His own life in order to save mine and all of humanity, the least I can do, is be obedient and give Him mine. All of me. And that sometimes means going out on a limb, beyond my comfort zone.

I haven't told a lot of people that I was writing this book. But a couple of my close friends whom I did tell, have asked me if I was nervous or scared because I could be setting myself up for failure. I certainly appreciate my friends concern, but I can honestly say I'm not looking at it that way because I didn't write this book for personal success, fame or money. And I'm certainly not expecting it to be on the New York Times Best-Sellers list or anything of the sort.

I think if I was going into it for my own personal glory, then yes, I'd be ridiculously nervous and scared. But knowing wholeheartedly that I wrote this for God's Glory and His alone, I can confidently rest in knowing it is all up to Him. It is He who will determine the outcome of this book and the ones who will read it.

Like I said before, I never in a million years would have guessed I'd be writing a book. It was only done out of obedience to God prompting me to share my excitement of a new and improved life that only He can offer. So whether I sell one or one thousand, it doesn't matter. What is most important is if you are the one person who does read it, you should know that God personally hand-picked and lovingly chose you to draw closer to Him—and you must understand, there truly is no greater honor. You are a chosen one. And if you are that one person, then that is enough for me to know my mission was accomplished.

As it is written in Luke 15:8-10, Jesus explains to his disciples The Parable of the Lost Coin: "Or what woman who has ten silver coins and loses one of them does not light a lamp, sweep her house, and search carefully until she finds it? And when she finds it, she calls together her friends and neighbors to say, 'Rejoice with me, for I have found my lost coin.' In the same way, I tell you, there is joy in the presence of God's angels over one sinner who repents."

Chapter 17

SUPERHERO vs. SAVIOR

When I became a Christian in 2008, I would always talk to my daughter about God and she had memorized The Lord's Prayer from the time she was two years old. I was a single mom and barely able to make ends meet. I vividly remember a certain situation that forced me to explain to her that no matter what, we were going to be okay because we now have God looking over us, to help us and protect us when we need it. She looked up at me with her big green eyes and said, "Wow, mommy, so Jesus is like a superhero!"

I paused, and with a big smile said, "Yes sweetie, you're right, He is like a superhero, but even better!" "Because superheroes are fictitious, and Jesus is real!"

We all desire someone to come to our rescue in a time of need. Or perhaps someone to save us in a life-or-death situation, whether it is a doctor during surgery or a paramedic at the scene of an accident. Yes, this is what we all hope for in a serious time of need. But again, even if our life or someone else's life is saved, isn't it still just temporary? A buying of time, so to speak?

Always remember, life is like the morning fog—here for a little while, then it's gone. Please think about all I have written and take it from someone who was once in your shoes not that long ago. It's Jesus, and Him alone, who provides that one true 'fix' we are all looking for. The difference is though, more than just a temporary 'fix', His is the CURE which is everlasting and eternal.

The Pharisees asked Jesus which of the Ten Commandments was most important. Jesus' response was to love God above all else, and secondly, to love our neighbor as ourselves. This statement is quite profound. When He is saying 'neighbor', He obviously isn't only referring to the person we live next door to. He is referring to the entire human race. If we were to love God first and love one another second, then the other eight commandments would fade into the background—we'd be filled with so much love toward one another that we wouldn't even be capable of disobeying the other eight Commandments.

So if the God of the universe could willingly leave His heavenly throne, come to earth in human form, and humble Himself to that level, then who the heck are we? Who do we think we are? In line at the grocery store, or even driving on the road, I see people all the time getting annoyed and impatient with others. I, myself struggle with this! We are all living with the 'me first' mind-set. But if we thought about it for a second, and do in a small way, as Jesus did, and put someone else's needs before our own, just think of how amazing this world would be.

Could you only imagine? How good does it feel when you help someone in need? Then why is it we only do this once in a while, instead of all the time? The answer is simple; because for the most part, we can't seem to find the time, or we don't see it as a priority, or we are too self-absorbed, too selfish and filled with *Spiritual Cancer*.

This *Spiritual Cancer* then blinds us to the need that is all around us. We all have an innate sense that there is something more than what the eye can see. However, since we do not see it, we often fail to believe in it. If we don't believe in it, then we cannot be aware of all that is going on—for and against us. Whether we choose to believe in the existence of spiritual beings and places or not, still does not change the fact of their existence and their activities. Let's step back for a minute to assess what we do believe.

We know that when we wake up every morning, our feet will hit the floor and gravity will keep us from floating away. Or if we toss a ball up into the air, pending no obstruction, we know it will come back down. Therefore, we have faith in gravity. We cannot 'see' gravity, but we know it exists. Faith too is invisible. I read a quote once that said: "God is like oxygen. You can't see Him, but you need Him to survive."

As Christians, we have blind faith to believe in Jesus Christ. We cannot physically see Him, but we believe that He died on the cross for our sins. We believe that God raised Him from the dead, and we believe that He alone is the source of our eternal salvation. We believe Jesus accomplished these things in the spiritual realm when He lived in the physical realm on earth.

We know that we, too, need to believe in this physical realm to be welcomed into His spiritual realm. Thus, it is blind faith that confirms to our hearts that we will be going to a very real place called Heaven someday. The Bible is filled with references to the heavenly realm—a place that is invisible to our eyes today, yet very real in its existence. We believe with the eyes of our heart, instead of the eyes in our head.

But unfortunately, our pride sometimes gets in the way and we can be too egotistical to rely on someone else. Or, I can admit, it's hard to put faith in something or someone we cannot see. Plus, it's obviously not 'cool' to worship a guy who many of us picture as wearing a long white robe, with a glowing halo over His head and walking around with His hands held together in prayer. So what if I told you Jesus looked like Superman—a massive 6'8" man with jacked-up muscles? Or what if He was the greatest football, baseball or basketball player—times a thousand? Would it be easier to worship Him then? We certainly worship and idolize our fair share of sports stars, don't we? We idolize them based on their superior performance. So, based on all the supernatural miracles Jesus performed, isn't it safe to say that He is far more worthy of our praise and worship than anyone else?

The point is, no one, to this day, knows exactly what Jesus looked like. We've certainly seen many different portrayals, but the truth remains, no one knows for sure. He wasn't around during the time of cameras, social media and selfies. So, we can speculate and imagine all we want, but no one knows for sure. And here's the thing; God planned it this way. He didn't want us to idolize Jesus based on His looks and stature. He wanted us to trust and believe in Him based on His words and His actions alone.

Now ask yourself, who's really the strong one? The one living life like everyone else by society's norm, or the one who sets themselves apart from the rest? How difficult is it to be different nowadays? It's so much easier to follow the norm. We typically do what it takes to fit in and be like everyone else.

How hard would it be to step back and surrender control of your life? It's probably one of the hardest things I've ever done. It requires humility. It requires trust. It requires blind faith. All of these, by the way, are predicated on having the utmost strength—inner strength. It would be so much easier to live life like the majority who work, schedule, plan, organize, and repeat—going about their daily lives, doing the same ritualistic things day in and day out. These things that occupy our time make us feel like we have purpose. So to surrender this control would be one of the most difficult tasks of all. It strips us of our so-called power to control. Yet true strength, real strength and the greatest strength comes from a person who allows themselves to be vulnerable. Only a very strong person can let go and let God.

Imagine yourself as a toddler and you're walking through a huge crowd of people at the biggest football event of the year—the Superbowl. The arena is jam-packed with people and because you are so small, you cannot see anything except people's bodies crowded all around you and it makes you feel uneasy. But in that moment, your Dad reaches down and grabs your hand. You know He loves you and doesn't want anything bad to happen to you. So you blindly trust that he will protect and guide you since he can see above all the people and the chaos and has a clear view of where you are going. It gives you great peace and comfort knowing he is navigating you safely through the crowd to get you where you need to go.

God is no different. He has a birds-eye view from His Heavenly perspective. He sees above all the chaos in our lives and all we need to do is be like the toddler, just reach our hands up to grab His and blindly trust Him to navigate for us.

The world promises instant gratification and pleasures that fulfill the desires of our flesh—a tempting offer, but only temporary fixes. When we die, no matter how successful we are or how much money we make, none of it can be taken with us. The things of this earth become meaningless when compared to eternity in heaven with our mighty Creator! How freeing is that, as 1 Peter 2:9 tells us, "This world is not our home." There is obviously more out there than just this world we live in and the world we see.

And speaking of money, it wasn't that long ago when I believed that churches were only after our money and to be honest, it really bothered me. But here is what I've come to realize. God cares more about our hearts than our wallets. He doesn't need our money. He's the one who created money. Everything belongs to Him anyway. We are merely his money managers.

After my India experience, when I first became a believer, I was a single mother barely able to make ends meet. I remember digging up some loose change from the floor of my car just to buy diapers for my daughter. Although I didn't have much money at the time, what I did have was a strong desire to give something, even though it was a small amount, to my church, in return for the greatest gift God had just given me. I felt zero pressure and zero obligation. This was done solely out of my own personal desire. My heart was so overflowing with joy and gratitude, I felt it was the least I could do.

Then, as I began to read my Bible and draw closer to God, I later read the following scripture in Luke 21:1-4 which tells of a poor widow's offering, "While Jesus was in the Temple, he watched the rich people dropping their gifts in the collection box. Then a poor widow came by and dropped in two small coins. "I tell you the truth," Jesus said, "this poor widow has given more than all the rest of them. For they have given a tiny part of their wealth, but she, poor as she is, has given everything she has."

I had heard that the Bible was referred to as God's *living word* and it was as if God Himself was speaking directly to me in this passage. The bottom line is this; giving should come from our hearts because we have a desire to give, not because we feel obligated. This is another one of those choices that lies solely between you and God.

If we hear the term tithe in church, it typically refers to giving a tenth or just ten percent of our income. We get to keep the rest - the ninety percent. Again, this is everyone's personal choice. But whatever we are prompted to give, whether it be ten percent, or more, or less, whatever it is, we are making an investment in eternity, which is better than any investment we can make in the stock market or anywhere else here on earth. As it is written in Matthew 6:19-21, "Do not store up for yourselves treasures on earth, where moths and vermin destroy, and where thieves break in and steal. But store up for yourselves treasures in heaven, where moths and vermin do not destroy, and where thieves do not break in and steal. For where your treasure is, there your heart will be also."

God sees a person's heart and He will always bless those that give cheerfully. As it says in 2 Corinthians 9:6-7, "The point is this: who-ever sows sparingly will also reap sparingly, and whoever sows bountifully will also reap bountifully. Each one must give as he has decided in his heart, not reluctantly or under compulsion, for God loves a cheerful giver." It is important to know and trust the church or place you are giving money (tithing) to. The reason we tithe is so we can be a part of advancing God's Kingdom. To share God's love and the Good News with others.

Our church, LifeChurch, for example, uses the money we all give, for building new church locations, the fulfillment of their *Switch* ministry (which is specifically designed for teens), donating to international crisis relief, partnering with local charities, as well as the ongoing development of their YouVersion Bible App.

Not everyone has access to a Bible and because of our giving, we have helped make it possible for LifeChurch to offer 2,027 Bible versions in 1,355 different languages for free. This YouVersion Bible App is very interactive and helps a person stay connected daily in order to strengthen and build an intimate relationship with God.

Another great free app is the DailyBible app which is very simple and straightforward. Bible.is is a dramatized audio Bible app where each chapter of the Bible is read by different people/voices, along with sound-effects and background music, making you feel like you're there within the pages. I personally like listening to this while I'm getting ready in the morning, driving in my car or at night before bed. This is where technology meets the current needs of our busy lives by helping us stay connected while on the go.

All I can say is, I have seen and experienced the benefits of a relationship with God and would love nothing more than for you to experience this as well. God's gifts are far greater than anything else we can imagine and are filled with more love, joy, and peace than what the world offers. And this is something no amount of money can buy.

No matter how old you are, no matter how long you think you've been doing things on your own, no matter how much control you think you have, no matter how good or bad life is going for you, no matter what your circumstances are, God is there for you, and He can and will make your life even better. His desire is to help you in every aspect of your life, even in the smallest of details.

I mentioned previously King David, who when he was a small boy, killed Goliath the giant with just a slingshot and stone. David had strong faith and trusted in God's mighty power. So no matter how big, or giant our problems may seem, we must have faith like David to believe the following: The giant in front of you is never bigger than the God inside of you.

Our human idea of strength and God's idea of strength are at complete odds with one another. God says as much in 2 Corinthians 12:9 says, "My strength is made perfect in weakness." The Apostle Paul, to whom this is attributed, was able to see clearly and freely admit his own weakness and was willing to get himself out of the way so God could then take over and work. He realized that if he tried to do God's will in his own strength, he would fail and come up short every time. Wouldn't it be easier and better for us all, knowing we don't have to work things out using our own efforts?

It takes a much stronger person to realize this and let go of the control. In the Old Testament, God continually told the leaders of Israel to reduce the size of their armies, and sometimes He would announce in advance how their victory would be won. Why? So they would not place their trust in their own strength and, instead, see first-hand God at work and learn to trust in Him. I once heard a saying: "God's work, done in God's way, will never lack for God's provision." It's a statement so obvious and yet so easily ignored.

Think back to when you were about eight years old and you grabbed an unopened pickle jar from the refrigerator. Your mom saw you struggling as you tried to open it and said, "Hey sweetie, let me help you with that." Now, did you gladly hand it over, knowing she could easily open it for you, or did you stubbornly say, "No, no, I got it!" and continue to struggle with it as you became more and more frustrated? How much easier was it to just hand the jar to your mom and have her open it for you?

Again, God is the same. When He sees us struggling, He strongly desires to help us. He loves us and is looking for receptive followers. Receptivity opens your innermost being to be filled with God's abundant blessings. Be attentive and direct your attention toward God. Ask Him for help in all situations. Search for Him in every moment. By doing this, you will be pleasantly surprised at how much easier and joyful life will become as you experience His help, guidance and perfect peace.

No longer do we need to see bad circumstances as a bad thing. I now whole-heartedly trust His purpose and plan for my life so that even in the bad times, I know He is right there by my side, guiding me through. Trials are no longer trials when you know there is a greater meaning and purpose behind them.

And I have certainly been through enough bad times in my life to now look back and see there has always been a silver lining. Always. God has always been there working behind the scenes. And the sooner we turn to God for help and surrender control, the quicker He can work to resolve and help us through any given situation.

Strangely enough, I am thankful that troubles highlighted my dependence and need for God. God's strength is revealed much more brilliantly in our helplessness. I've lived the lesson of James 1: 2-4, "Dear brothers and sisters, when troubles of any kind come your way, consider it an opportunity for great joy. For you know that when your faith is tested, your endurance has a chance to grow. So let it grow, for when your endurance is fully developed, you will be perfect and complete, needing nothing."

Life without God can feel like being stranded in the middle of the ocean, treading water, gasping for air, struggling to keep your head above water as the waves of life continually pummel you. Now picture yourself again stranded in the middle of the ocean, but this time you are at least sitting comfortably and protected within a large, indestructible life raft. You're still getting hit by the same waves as before, but now you have a safe and trustworthy barrier of protection.

That, my dear friends, is a life with God and is the beauty of a relationship with Christ.

What an honor it is for a football team to win the Superbowl or for someone to have their name written on a star in the Hollywood Walk of Fame. Sure, those things are great, but they're temporary. To receive either would be an amazing honor, especially in the moment, but as days and weeks go by, they would soon be forgotten by many and certainly nothing that is of any use daily. But this relationship with our Mighty Creator is not only the highest of all honors but is something we can utilize and count on daily and will continue to grow, develop and strengthen from now into eternity.

Take it from me—I spent the first 37 years of my life without God. I am a strong, stubborn, independent soul and it took me a very long time to finally see the light. In most cases, God will lovingly, patiently and persistently keep tapping a person on the shoulder, giving subtle cues to get their attention. However, in my case, because I'm a fighter, I had to be emotionally knocked down, hit upside the head and dragged through the mud before I was willing to surrender emotionally. But I cannot tell you how glad I am that I finally did, because it has been beyond worth it!

I've now had the honor and privilege of spending the past 12 years with Him and counting. This is something I am so grateful for and so proud of. Religion carries the stigma of something that should be private or is sometimes looked down upon, or perhaps causes a certain level of embarrassment when discussing with other people. But this book is not about religion. It is about a relationship—a relationship to be proud of. Who wouldn't want a real-life superhero to count on? Who wouldn't be proud of this and want to share this amazing gift with others? It is the greatest honor that anyone could receive.

Many people will say they believe in God or some higher power. Even the Bible tells us in *James 2:19*,*"You say you have faith, for you believe that there is one God. Good for you! Even the demons believe this, and they tremble in terror."* But believing is just part of the equation. Christianity is so much more than just a 'belief' in a higher power—it is transformational. When you enter into this relationship with Jesus, He will then transform and change your life for the better.

Like all relationships, it's reciprocal and dynamic. It's not just an ethereal belief that there may be some higher power out there; rather you will experience first-hand a powerful God who has the power to transform your life.

We all know life can be difficult at times. Sure, things can go great for a period of time, but there will always be periods of bad times as well. These are unavoidable. We live in a fallen, broken world, and life for us here on earth will never be perfect. We are human, we are flawed and imperfect, and we will always let each other down. We are incapable of being the person others want us to be. This certainly doesn't sound like we're operating from a position of strength now does it?

It is God who provides us hope and strength. And it is our hope, faith and trust in God's promises—that He will sustain and help us during those difficult times that gives us that strength, assurance and confidence. He promises to be there for us 100 percent of the time. Although we may not physically see Him, we take comfort in knowing He is there, working out our lives on our behalf.

God surely has answered enough of my prayers and performed enough miracles in my life to prove He is real. And I (and those who know me) can visibly see the remarkable difference and huge blessings in my life compared to what my life used to be. As it says in Philippians 4:13, "I can do all things through Christ who gives me strength." I no longer need to be strong on my own. I now have God's supernatural strength to draw upon.

There is a great example in the Book of John, Chapter 8, where we are told about a woman caught in the act of adultery. The law at that time stated that any person caught in adultery was to be stoned to death, no questions asked. The Pharisees and religious leaders who despised Jesus, were continually asking loaded questions and testing Him in order to find something they could use against Him. In this particular instance, the Pharisees brought the adulterous woman into the middle of a crowd where Jesus was teaching in an attempt to trap Him once and for all.

Here is how it played out in John 8: 4-11, "Teacher," they said to Jesus, "this woman was caught in the act of adultery. The law of Moses says to stone her. What do you say?" They were trying to trap him into saying something they could use against him, but Jesus stooped down and wrote in the dust with his finger. They kept demanding an answer, so he stood up again and said, "All right, but let the one who has never sinned throw the first stone!" Then he stooped down again and wrote in the dust. When the accusers heard this, they slipped away one by one, beginning with the oldest, until only Jesus was left in the middle of the crowd with the woman. Then Jesus stood up again and said to the woman, "Where are your accusers? Didn't even one of them condemn you?" "No, Lord," she said. And Jesus said, "Neither do I. Go and sin no more."

This story is so powerful and moving. And there are many others like this written within the pages of The Bible. It is beautiful to see how calm, wise, sensible, loving and gracious Jesus' response is in every situation. He dealt so lovingly and tenderly with every sinful (imperfect) person. The ones who screwed up. The ones who made mistakes. The ones the Pharisees and religious leaders wanted to condemn! That is our God; our superhero, our savior, in action.

A God who protects, who does not judge or condemn and who shows His true heart and love for us. Our God exemplified. His teachings are always perfect and on point. I love how the ones who appeared and tried to be perfect were the ones Jesus put in their place with His words of wisdom. As much as the Pharisees tried to test Jesus on numerous occasions, it always backfired. Which inevitably angered them even more.

There never has been, nor will there ever be a more popular person with such controversy surrounding Him. Why? Because He clearly had to be who He said He was. If we all could stop passing judgment and just spend a little time getting to know Him and what He came to do, we would soon realize that He is who He said He was —God in the flesh. Don't you love watching a movie when you already know the good guy wins in the end?

Well, that is the same case here. Jesus—the one and only true superhero—has already won the war against evil. He has already crushed Satan (the bad guy) beneath His feet and provides the end all, be all cure for the one thing that infects the entire human race— *Spiritual Cancer*.

In the days we live in, not everyone can be trusted, and the world is sometimes filled with fear and hatred. But what a gift of security to know that we can have confidence in the strength and power of the One who has already conquered evil, once and for all. Why would we turn our backs and refuse to believe in His mighty existence?

He is patiently waiting for each and every one of us to turn our attention toward Him, put our faith in Him, and to trust Him in any situation. Because no matter what, He's got our backs. We can live with confidence knowing that outside forces like the media, our peers and events beyond our control are not to be feared. As it says in 1 John 4:18, "There is no fear in love, but perfect love casts out fear. For fear has to do with punishment, and whoever fears has not been perfected in love." When you give yourself over to God, fear loses all its power. His perfect love in our lives casts out all our fears; fear of the future, fear of the unknown, fear of death, fear of anything and everything.

It makes me sad now when God gets such a bad rap. There are so many misconceptions floating around out there and I used to be one who contributed to those misconceptions. But now, my desire is to set the record straight. He is the exact opposite of what I used to think and what the masses think.

Picture the greatest best friend or best parental figure a person could possibly have. Someone who truly is perfect. Someone you can tell everything to, someone you can trust one hundred percent of the time with anything and everything, someone who can supernaturally help you out in any and all situations, someone you can cast your cares and burdens on, someone who can provide you peace and comfort when you're worried or stressed, someone who can guide or direct you with decisions (both big and small), someone who will never fail you, someone who always has your best interest and always knows what's best for you.

One of the first scriptures I taught my daughter at a very young age is Romans 8:31, "...If God is for us, who can ever be against us?" Especially with all the bullying that goes on today, every child, teenager and adult should know; if our All-Mighty, All-Powerful

God is for us, no mere person can be against us. Wow! What is better than that? This is a strong foundation of truth we can all stand on.

So tell me, who wouldn't want someone like this in their life? Someone we can count on and who has our backs. Wouldn't this be a dream come true? The best news of all is this person does exist and is real and can be there for you in an instant. Psalm 18:2 tells us, "The LORD is my rock, my fortress, and my savior; my God is my rock, in whom I find protection. He is my shield, the power that saves me, and my place of safety."

Today is the perfect time to put this hope and faith into action. This Coronavirus is highly contagious and continues to spread like wildfire. It has clearly exposed human vulnerability. In a time like this, it becomes apparent that we all have been living our lives with a false sense of security. Our daily schedules, priorities, projects and habits all become trivial and meaningless in a time like this and it goes to show what little control we have. These truly are depressing, sad, and uncertain times.

Yet, as tragic and scary as this is, I know that God has a plan and has complete control of this. And I trust that somehow, someway, it will all be okay and that this too will have a silver lining.

But now is the time, especially with all the racial injustice and social unrest, for us to unite as one nation under God, one world under God, and do our part—turn to Him and seek His help in this dire situation. We are all created in His image—all created equal.

Lecrae once again summed it up perfectly when he posted the following on his Instagram: "God is not a Republican or Democrat. God is not a conservative or a liberal. America is no more God's country than South Africa. God doesn't take sides. HE TAKES OVER.

No one in the world has the power to stop this virus, stop the hate and racism, or the power to get our lives and the economy back up and running. Only God can. He is our only hope. It's the year 2020, and we all know 20/20 is considered perfect vision. Perhaps God is using the year 2020 for us to see clearly, that as Creator of all, He has supreme control and He is the only one who can help us.

Like I said before, we have nothing to lose and everything to gain. There is no better time than the present. God is calling all of humanity back to Him. All it takes is simple prayer/dialog. Matthew

7:7-8 tells us, "Keep on asking, and you will receive what you ask for. Keep on seeking, and you will find. Keep on knocking, and the door will be opened to you. For everyone who asks, receives. Everyone who seeks, finds. And to everyone who knocks, the door will be opened."

This news I share with you is the greatest GOOD NEWS: the news that God loves you, He has a plan for your life, and He is patiently waiting for you to seek His help. He will forever be by your side no matter what and will bless you beyond measure if you can simply own up to your mistakes and then turn your focus toward Him for guidance. And most importantly, you will have eternity in glorious Heaven to look forward to, because there truly is more to this life than what we see. This is by far the greatest free gift anyone could ever receive.

If you and I were friends and I showed up at your house with a beautifully wrapped gift and was so excited to give it to you, would you turn away from me and refuse to accept it? Of course, you wouldn't. So why wouldn't you accept this free gift from our loving God in the same way—with open arms?

A friend once said to me: "Aren't you glad He's an: 'I don't care what you've done or how far you've run, just come home', kind of God!"

Having God by your side will provide a richly fulfilling life with immeasurable success. But keep in mind, success is not solely measured by money. True success is defined by your life as a whole. When you function in love, you will have a successful family, successful relationships, success with your job and you will experience supernatural peace and joy no matter what circumstances come your way. I can only say this because I am living it. And this is not specific or special to me. I am no different than you. We all must do our part by being transparent and sincere. We have to wholeheartedly seek and search for Him. He sees the true desires of our heart so we cannot fake it and we cannot do it half-way.

I remember thinking only weak people needed God and ironically, this is the case. Because the truth is, we are all weak, we are all fragile and it is only in our weakness and brokenness that we can find Him. Brokenness will look different for each of us and will come in varying degrees, but it's our brokenness that opens our hearts and minds up to being vulnerable. Brokenness causes desperation and desperation causes us to seek help. In brokenness, we let our guard down and a simple prayer or plea for help is all it takes. Only in our weakness and brokenness can we find Him.

He is our true superhero, our savior.

I heard a story describing each of us something like a pumpkin. God picks us from the patch, brings us in, and washes all the dirt off us. The outside is what we look like to others and what people see. The inside represents our soul and our heart, the part that only God sees. We all know how yucky the inside of a pumpkin is when we go to clean it out. A pumpkin left to itself will soon rot and die, just as we too will die someday.

God is the only one who can change our hearts. But for God to change our hearts, we must become open to Him. God is the only one who can clean out all the yucky stuff inside of us. He removes the seeds of doubt, hate, impurity, anger, fear, resentment, heartlessness, greed, jealousy and pride.

But if the pumpkin is left with just the insides taken out, then it's just hollow. We need to have a light inside that will truly make us alive! Jesus said in John 8:12, "I am the light of the world. Whoever follows me will never walk in darkness, but will have the light of life." When Jesus lives inside of you, you will glow! God then carves you a smiling face and puts His light inside of you to shine for all the world to see.

Every morning you wake up, is another day to be thankful for and another chance to make a change—a change for the better. Now that you've been educated and now that you're aware, then now is the time to ask and receive this cure for *Spiritual Cancer*. Just be honest with yourself and with God and ask Him for help. The quicker you ask, seek and knock, the quicker you can start to feel His supernatural peace and start to enjoy the life you were meant to have.

The stories mentioned in this book may be unique to me, but I can assure you that God has already written and woven your own unique stories within the tapestry of your life. He is just waiting patiently to share and reveal them to you. God has a special purpose and a plan just for you, so I encourage you to take that leap of faith and just give Him a chance.

I promise you will not be disappointed!

It's your turn to be that SPARK!

Why waste another day or even another moment living with the deadliest, most hidden disease of all:
Spiritual Cancer
We all could use a real-life superhero and savior right now, and it's as easy as calling on the One who can and will instantly cure you once and for all:

JESUS

Photo Credit: julian80 @deviantART.com

ENDNOTES:

1. http://www.osguinness.com/about-os-guinness/
2. https://www.rzim.org/read/just-thinking-magazine/why-truth-matters
3. Robert Jastrow; "Message from Professor Robert Jastrow"; *LeaderU.com;* 2002
4. Richard Feynman, *The Meaning of It All: Thoughts of a Citizen-Scientist* (New York: BasicBooks, 1998)
5. What is the source of the heat in Earth's interior? *Posted by* EarthSky *in* EARTH | September 6, 2010
6. Ibid
7. How Big is the Sun? | Size of the Sun By Tim Sharp November 01, 2017. Space.com
8. The Wonders of God's Creation, Moody Institute of Science (Chicago, IL)
9. Ibid.
10. The Wonders of God's Creation, Moody Institute of Science (Chicago, IL)
11. Francis S. Collins, director of the Human Genome Project, and author of *The Language of God,* (Free Press, New York, NY), 2006
12. God's Masterpiece by Joseph Paturi on September 1, 1998
13. The Wonders of God's Creation, Moody Institute of Science (Chicago, IL)
14. Hugh Davson, *Physiology of the Eye,* 5th ed (New York: McGraw Hill, 1991)
15. *Pedrosa, Marina. "Avril Lavigne Makes Powerful Comeback With Emotional Single 'Head Above Water': Listen". Billboard. Retrieved September 19, 2018.*
16. Deshpande, MS (ed) (1978) Light of India or Message of Mahatmaji, 3rd ed. Ahmedabad: Navajivan Publishing House
17. Gandhi, M.K. (1948): Non-Violence in Peace and War, Volume I, p. 181
18. ibid, Volume II, p. 166
19. ibid, Volume II, p. 16
20. Gandhi, M.K. (1955), My Religion, Compiled/edited by Bharatan Kumarappa, Ahmedabad: Navjivan Publishing House, p. 25
21. Gandhi, M.K. (1927): An Autobiography or The Story of My Experiments with Truth, Ahmedabad: Navjivan Publishing House, p. 22-23
22. ibid, p. 48
23. ibid, p. 49

ACKNOWLEDGEMENTS

To my husband, Varun (Timmy) Sharma: What can I say? You truly are my greatest gift, my grounding force, my voice of reason and my endless support. As you patiently listen to me when I'm doubting myself and ready to give up, you are always there to build me up and encourage me to continue on. You are my best friend, my love, my business partner and my rock! Thank you for not just believing in me but knowing I could do anything I set my heart and mind to! And I thank you for being an exceptional father to our daughter, ParisElla. I Love You Deeply, Forever and Always!

To my daughter, ParisElla: You are the best thing I have ever done in my life! You welcomed me into motherhood, and I am so grateful for you. You have blossomed into a beautiful young lady and I am beyond blessed to be your mom. Your sweet, kind and gentle soul always points out the good in any person or situation. Your Godly spirit is a light to my path. I have learned so much from you; my wise child. Always stay true to who you are in Christ and never conform to the norm. Be strong and proud to stand out and be different. Your light will always shine bright in this world. I look forward to seeing the big plans our Mighty Lord has in store for you my love!

I thank my sisters Donna and Debbie, my late father Kenneth and my late mother Margaret who adopted me into their family when I was one month old. You raised me as your own and loved and guided me to the best of your ability—because I know I wasn't easy!

To my biological mother Jeanne, whom I never had the privilege of meeting because her life was tragically and unexpectedly taken before I could find her; and to my biological father Andy – thank you both for giving me life! I am so grateful for you Andy and for my entire biological family who welcomed me into their lives with loving and open arms.

Thank you Marybeth Reilly McGreen for your professional guidance and expertise. It was no coincidence you came into my life when you did. This book took on a whole new life once you provided your input and ideas. You honestly know me better than I know myself—and for this I will be eternally grateful.

Thank you, Pastor Brian and Jenni Atkins, for providing not only a solid and meaningful friendship, but wise, valuable and honest advice and feedback. We love you and your beautiful family so very much and we are so very thankful for our entire LifeChurch family!

To my long-time friend Lena Uhren: you have been my GTG (go-to-girl) from the very beginning, as you patiently navigated me through this amazing faith journey. I am so grateful for you!

Jamie Dahl, you are a true inspiration, my beloved sister in Christ. It was your story and brave struggle with breast cancer that prompted my heart to write this book. I thank God for His saving grace in your life.

Thank you Moko and Tulsi for your grace and understanding. We love you both so very much!

A big thank you to Pastor Isaac Shaw, Gloria and your entire family for being our solid foundation in India. You have welcomed us into your family and have provided endless wisdom and advice to us as we have embarked upon unchartered waters. We will always be most grateful for your wise guidance and loving friendship.

Thank you Dr. Shepherd for being the wise, spiritual leader that you are for our Salvation Tree School. You have been a true blessing—shepherding our flock.

To all the women I have led, taught, and learned from in Bible Studies throughout the years. You all have been so special to me and I wouldn't be where I am today without you. I'd like to give special thanks to my Golden Girls (Patti & Geri) for being my biggest cheerleaders and Bonnie, Lisa, Rhonda, and Carol for always encouraging and believing in me.

Thank you Jess Fronrath for your shared passion for Jesus. I always love and cherish our lengthy, Godly discussions.

Annette, Janemarie, Lorianne, Melody, Darcey, Tracey, Patty and Maria, I am so blessed by all of you.

Cindy Cruciotti and Kelli Cruciotti-Vanderveen—you both have been such a blessing and a true answer to prayer—helping me attain my equestrian goals and making dreams come true. You are remarkable trainers and I love and appreciate you both so much. And a big thank you to Andres for being a very important part of our family and our team. As the saying goes; *Teamwork Makes the Dream Work!*

And most importantly, I would like to thank the number one Man in my life. My Lord and Savior, The One and Only, King of Kings and Lord of Lords, who needs no further introduction: Jesus Christ!!! Seriously, I still cannot believe how real You are. My mind and thoughts instinctively speak with you daily and it amazes me how You answer even the most trivial of prayers. You may take your time answering some of them, but I know and completely trust that your timing is perfect. One of my favorite verses is found in *Matthew 19:26, "..with God, all things are possible.."* and this book is proof of that. Coming from a woman who had NEVER read a book from cover to cover, despised reading and writing in school and used Cliffs Notes to write my book reports, clearly writing this book was not my doing. So I thank you Lord, for taking a hot-mess like me and transforming my life in such a beautiful way.

And I am thankful for YOU, my reader. If you are the ONE that is willing to take that leap of faith and give Jesus a chance, then I'd love to hear about it! I am so excited for you and your new life's journey!

ABOUT THE AUTHOR

Laurie Sharma has been blessed with a true entrepreneurial and philanthropic mind and spirit and gives Jesus all the credit for everything she has and does. She is the co-owner and designer of the USA equestrian brands: Equine Couture, TuffRider and Henri de Rivel. She and her husband Timmy have factories in India which also manufacture and private label for other major equestrian brands globally. Laurie and Timmy own the equestrian lifestyle brand JUMP USA. Laurie has been able to adapt her equestrian design ideas into everyday apparel, making JUMP USA one of the leading retail online brands throughout India. And because of her love for animals, she has also designed a line of fashionable dog collars under the brand Halo.

Nearest and dearest to Laurie's heart is her Salvation Tree School based in Greater Noida, India, which she and Timmy founded in 2010 to provide free education to the children of their factory employees. They recently purchased two and a half acres of land and have built a much larger, state-of-the-art school facility. Their desire was to expand their efforts and welcome more than just the children of their employees and now they are able to accommodate nearly 2000 children. Proceeds from this book will go toward their school in India in hopes that they will have the financial means to build many more Salvation Tree Schools in the coming years.

Laurie has taught and led Bible Studies for over 6 years and has a strong passion for educating people with her new-found faith and the true reality of Jesus. She is living proof of how He can remarkably and supernaturally transform lives beyond anyone's wildest imagination.

She and her team are currently in the process of creating a new series of conferences and events called the BURN movement, (Believers Unite to Revive Nations).

Laurie splits her time between India and the USA where she enjoys life as a wife and mother. She spends her free time riding horses and competing in equestrian show jumping competitions in Wellington, FL where she, Timmy and their daughter ParisElla live on their equestrian property alongside their four-legged family consisting of horses, dogs and cats. To find out more, go to:

- LaurieSharma.com
- SpiritualCancer.com
- SalvationTree.edu.in
- EquineCouture.com
- Breeches.com
- JumpUSA.in
- BURNmvmt.com

CONTEMPORARY CHRISTIAN MUSIC PICKS

Below is a list of my own personal favorite Contemporary Christian Music picks. There are so many more great songs and artists, but these in particular have either raised my spirits to the point I'm up and dancing (my daily theme song is "Joy", by For King & Country) or they spoke to me in such a way that moved me to tears—happy tears! Either way, each one of these songs is special to me. I may not be a gambling woman, but I can almost bet at least one of these songs will somehow speak to you:

TobyMac:
"I just need U."
"Move"
"Speak Life"
"Til The Day I Die"
"Lose My Soul" (ft. Mandisa)
"Love Broke Through"
"Scars"

Austin French:
"Why God"

Avril Lavigne
"Head Above Water"
"Fly"

Big Daddy Weave:
"Alive"
"My Story"
"Audience Of One"

Brandon Heath:
"Give Me Your Eyes"

Britt Nicole:
"The Lost Get Found"

Casting Crowns:	"Already There"
	"Great Are Your Lord"
Chasen:	"Drown"
Chris Tomlin:	"Our God"
Colton Dixon:	"More of You"
Cory Asbury:	"Reckless Love"
For King & Country:	"Joy"
	"God Only Knows"
	"Shoulders"
	"The Proof Of Your Love"
Hannah Kerr:	"Warrior"
Hawk Nelson:	"Crazy Love"
Hillsong:	"Touch The Sky"
	"Oceans"
Hollyn:	"Alone" (ft. TRU)
Jason Gray:	"Glow In The Dark"
Jeremy Camp:	"The Way"
	"There Will Be A Day"
	"Same Power"
	"Dead Man Walking"
	"Understand"

Jesus Culture **(feat. Chris Quilala):**	"Fierce"
Jordan Feliz:	"The River"
Josh Baldwin:	"Stand In Your Love"
Lauren Daigle:	"You Say" "First"
Lecrae:	"I'll Find You" (ft. Tory Kelly) "Tell The World" (ft. Mali Music) "Blessings" (ft. Ty Dolla $ign)
Passion Feat. Kristian Stanfill:	"Even So Come" "One Thing Remains"
Mat Kearney:	"Face To Face" "Air I Breathe"
MercyMe:	"I Can Only Imagine" (From the Title Movie) "You Are I Am" "Here With Me"
Newsboys:	"God's Not Dead" "Born Again"
Plumb:	"Hang On"
Seabird:	"Don't' You Know You're Beautiful"

Skillet:	"Stars" "Lions"
Superchick:	"We Live" "Stand In The Rain"
Switch:	"Symphony"
Switchfoot:	"Dare You To Move" "This Is Your Life" "Native Tongue"
Tenth Avenue North:	"You are More" "What You Want" "By Your Side" "Hold My Heart" "Control"
The Afters:	"Light Up The Sky" "Every Good Thing"
Zach Williams:	"No Longer Slaves"

www.ingramcontent.com/pod-product-compliance
Lightning Source LLC
Chambersburg PA
CBHW062205080426
42734CB00010B/1802